# Pushing the Envelope

# Pushing the Envelope
## Epistolary Poems

Edited by

Jonas Zdanys

LAMAR UNIVERSITY
LITERARY PRESS

ISBN: 978-0-9915321-5-5
Library of Congress Control Number: 2015931098

Manufactured in the United States

Lamar University Press
Beaumont, Texas

# Acknowledgments

Some of the poems in this collection were previously published in the following journals and anthologies.

*Cha: An Asian Literary Journal*
*Contemporary Bestiary*
*Dream Diary*
*Manzanita Quarterly*
*mind the gaps*
*Mixed Blessings*
Strange Borderlands
*The Comstock Review*
*Wild River Review*
*Word Tech*
*World Literature Today*

## Poetry from Lamar University Literary Press

Alan Berecka, *With Our Baggage*

David Bowles, *Flower, Song, Dance: Aztec and Mayan Poetry*

Jerry Bradley, *Crownfeathers and Effigies*

Paul Christensen, *The Jack of Diamonds is a Hard Card to Play*

Chip Dameron, *Waiting for an Etcher*

William Virgil Davis, *The Bones Poems*

Jeffrey DeLotto, *Voices Writ in Sand*

Mimi Ferebee, *Wildfires and Atmospheric Memories*

Larry Griffin, *Cedar Plums*

Ken Hada, *Margaritas and Redfish*

Michelle Hartman, *Disenchanted and Disgruntled*

Michelle Hartman, *Irony and Irreverence*

Katherine Hoerth, *Goddess Wears Cowboy Boots*

Lynn Hoggard, *Motherland*

Gretchen Johnson, *A Trip Through Downer, Minnesota*

Ulf Kirchdorfer, *Chewing Green Leaves*

Janet McCann, *The Crone at the Casino*

Erin Murphy, *Ancilla*

Laurence Musgrove, *Local Bird*

Dave Oliphant, *The Pilgrimage, Selected Poems: 1962-2012*

Kornelijus Platelis, *Solitary Architectures*

Carol Coffee Reposa, *Underground Musicians*

Jan Seale, *The Parkinson Poems*

Carol Smallwood, *Water, Earth, Air, Fire, and Picket Fences*

Glen Sorestad *Hazards of Eden*

W.K. Stratton, *Ranchero Ford/ Dying in Red Dirt Country*

Wally Swist, *Invocation*

For information on Lamar University Press books go to
www.LamarUniversityPress.Org

For everyone who has mailed a poem in
an envelope

# CONTENTS

# II. Received

# Introduction

Letters in all their forms have been written and exchanged since our earliest days as members of communities, societies, and cultures. Historical records note that ancient populations—in India, Egypt, Greece, Rome, and China—used various kinds of correspondence, both within their boundaries and linking to the outside world, to communicate, to solicit information, to begin and track business matters, and to provide particulars in the conduct of relations with other individuals and groups. Written messages, thoughtfully conceived and carefully prepared, gave seriousness and dimension to all those matters, providing specific details so that those who wrote and read the letters could share an understanding of what was being agreed. Letters and other documents helped mitigate capricious response and provided frameworks for individuals and institutions to behave appropriately with one another, if at least on the surface.

The writing of letters has not only been a vehicle for personal or institutional relationships and not only a part of a constructed foundation for social and cross-cultural economic and political order. Letters have served broad and essential formative purposes as well. The Epistles of St. Paul, for example, are among the earliest documents of the Christian church. They were written as letters by Paul a few years after his conversion—scholars believe they were created about 50-60 A.D.—as explanations and exhortations to the Romans, Corinthians, Ephesians, Thessalonians and other communities to accept the teachings of Jesus. Those letters are essential to the formation of Christian theology and ethics and groundwork for the establishment of Christianity. Their philosophical and theological currents proved that writing which was directed to an audience, in its modulation of tone and through its beckoning voice, and through its presentation of new elevated ideas, could help to shape spectrums of reflection and belief.

The sense of beauty and philosophical depth that letters could provide, as the Pauline Epistles demonstrated, were gracefully affirmed and broadened some three hundred years later in the Byzantine Empire. In the fourth century, a new genre of literature flourished in Constantinople and other parts of the Eastern Roman Empire. It is now referred to as "epistolography," the art of writing letters. As historians Arnold Jones and Alexander Kazhdan (especially in his comprehensive *Oxford Dictionary of Byzantium)* have explained, the intellectual elite of the Empire perfected the form of the literary letter, using it not to provide information or to create treatises or to encourage theological connection but rather to savor the elegance of the writing itself. The letter became an art form, an object of beauty, where earlier practical considerations were replaced by aesthetic enjoyment. Letters, for some writers experimenting with that epistolographic form, became literary texts. Delight in their creation and in their reading was just as important as, and perhaps more important than, the instructions and information those texts may have provided.

Letters, of course, have also been part of literary texts for centuries. They are incorporated into epics and narratives and novels from the earliest days and are mentioned as far back as Homer. We often see, for example, a letter delivered or discovered that changes the course of a novel or a play and brings rise or fall to the characters who write or receive it. It is a deliberate and convenient literary device. In some cases, letters form the very structure of the novels themselves. These epistolary novels, which were especially popular during the 18<sup>th</sup> century, are texts where the author uses created letters as the entire frame, through them providing a variety of points of view and giving the reader the closest connection possible to what a character is thinking and feeling without succumbing to the need for what can sometimes be an obtrusive omniscient narrator. Samuel Richardson's *Pamela, or Virtue Rewarded* is a principal example and, some argue, the first novel written in English. Its significance, in this instance, is that the letters of which it is made both teach and delight the reader and take on strong aesthetic dimensions on their own accord. In many ways, they continue the predilections and expectations of the earlier epistolographic traditions.

Such literary letters appear in verse form as well. Roman poet

2

Ovid's *The Heroines* (or *Letters of Heroines*) is considered to be the first collection of epistolary poetry. That volume is a group of fifteen poems written in the form of letters by Ovid in the voices of various Greek and Roman mythological heroines—among them Penelope, Dido, Sappho, Ariadne, and Medea—who are unhappy about the ways in which they have been treated by men. Ovid, in fact, announced in his collection that he had invented an entirely new literary form, an innovative aesthetic connection between poetry and epistle. Some scholars question the point, but there is no doubt that Ovid did indeed use, if not fully invent, a new framework to connect with his audience, which he believed would be principally Roman women who may themselves have felt equally mistreated and who may have heard familiar voices in his epistolary couplets.

A quick scan across the centuries since Ovid notes other practitioners of the epistolary form, but not many of them. Various other poetic frameworks and directions appear to have been far more popular, perhaps especially as lyric poetry has evolved into such a dominant form, though important epistolary poetic works do appear as far back as the 9th century (a treatise on nothingness and darkness written in Latin by an Anglo-Saxon monk) and ranging into various individual collections in the 20th century.

It is in these interstices of letter and literature, of poem and epistle, that this volume finds its roots. This collection provides a look at the epistolary poem as it is being written today, in the early years of the 21st century. The poems here continue a long letter writing tradition, some two thousand years old, and while they may not be breaking new ground in terms of the structural connections they provide and consider between art and epistle, they do gather together distinctive voices and personal explorations of the form that, I hope, can give us additional insights and provide angles of reflection as to what is possible in this poetic epistolography. They do, I think, as the title suggests, in many ways push the literary envelope.

Most of the poems in this volume have been written expressly for it. Those that appeared first and just recently elsewhere are acknowledged. For this reason, this volume does not aim to be comprehensive, though the writers and their contributions have come from across the United States, and some have come from Canada, Europe, and Israel. It was not my intention to create a

3

handbook of epistolary poetry in general or of contemporary epistolary poetry as practiced across the globe. Rather, believing as I do that poetry provides us with a powerful insight into its moment, I gathered poems to provide a slice of what may be out there and to have this volume serve as both a reminder of and as a springboard for other collections. I also had something of an additional, perhaps secret, hope: that this collection might encourage others to consider writing this ancient literary form and to see whether it can continue to provide us with a clear and deep sense of immediacy of thought and experience that other poetic forms may have strayed away from. In this regard, I return to the notion that poetry, at its core, is communication, and perhaps considerations of poem-as-letter might reinforce that idea and help us move beyond the linguistic opacity of much of the poetry written today.

The poems in this collection address a wide range of matters, from the serious to the playful, from the formal to the idiosyncratic. The first section, which I have titled *Sent,* is a gathering of poetic letters of traditional epistolary form—that is, addressed to or meant for particular individuals—but which provide as well contemporary perspectives on political, familial, emotional, artistic, cultural, and historical elements and themes. The second section, titled *Received,* includes poems that reflect the writer's reaction— sometimes in the flash of an epiphanic moment—to what is contained inside an envelope that has been delivered or found. Some of these poems take the idea of "envelope" to a wider plane, and at least one of them considers the womb, for example, as the ultimate and primordial envelope. That envelope, as all of us who have children well know, surely contains surprises that redirect us when it opens and delivers the complex message inside.

It has been a privilege to discover that so many fine contemporary poets are writing epistolary poetry and considering craft as well as communication while doing so. The consideration of craft is, perhaps, especially salient today, when our various technologies often reduce ideas to quick bursts that provide information (though, I must admit, sometimes the abbreviations confuse me) but do not provide sufficient delight, do not engage either the sender or the receiver in the lovely textures of language that letters written by hand or by typewriter (and, perhaps, by word processing programs) once offered. The epistolary poems in this collection, I hope, give us information, linguistic texture, and aesthetic delight while both harkening back to earlier nuances and extensions of letter writing and looking ahead to contemporary immediacy.

For all these reasons, it has been a great pleasure to serve as the editor of this collection. This book began with an exchange of ideas and poems among members of the Virtual Artists Collective, a community so wonderfully guided by Steven Schroeder. I am grateful especially to Charlie Newman who initiated that exchange when he sent along a Kurt Vonnegut quote that triggered a wonderful responsive poetic dialogue about the idea and fact of "enveloping" as both noun and verb and that led me to consider in these pages how poems and letters are connected. The quote is as follows, taken from a PBS interview with Vonnegut:

> [When Vonnegut tells his wife he's going out to buy an envelope:] Oh, she says, well, you're not a poor man. You know, why don't you go online and buy a hundred envelopes and put them in the closet? And so I pretend not to hear her. And go out to get an envelope because I'm going to have a hell of a good time in the process of buying one envelope.

The idea of a single envelope, secured for a purpose, led naturally to the idea of what is inside it, and so this book took its shape as a look at what is sent and what is received and how poetry can explore both those dimensions. Jerry Craven of Lamar University Press was interested in such a dialogue and the possible literary result, which is this anthology, and I am grateful to him and to the Press for giving that initial early burst of poems a permanent home. I am grateful as well to J.C. Todd for her commitment to this book and for her active encouragement of so many to contribute so well, without which this anthology could not have come to closure. All of those who contributed their work to this collection have my deepest appreciation and admiration. I am delighted to be the steward of their energies and visions.

Jonas Zdanys
Sacred Heart University

# I. Sent

# Ascending the Mountain Slowly
### Walter Bargen

The first line to your letter forgotten as I sit down to respond.
The phone rings. Someone needs dried flowers for a vase in a room
      far away.
Her life doesn't yearn
for green, or something rooting through humus, groping around
      stones,
shoving aside all but water and light.

She wants what's left. Her room is all corners and walls. It's hard
      for her
to imagine more than the frail and brittle. Dried cockscomb,
      stiff baby's breath.
Perhaps something exotic and common
as the dry hiss of rattlesnake grass as she passes the table. Whatever
      opens
the room without opening the door.

Now I have forgotten the second and third lines of your letter.
I open the window beside the desk to hear the relentless chirring of
      cicadas
and their hard-bodied backup. It's the choking
of an engine in another season, their spring-loaded legs and unsteady
      wings
clicking and rasping. In the middle of the field the oak
a dying traffic jam.

More of your carefully crafted lines have died in the scalpeled
      schedule of silences.
Before I address what's left, as if I might suture sentences back
      together,
I notice the envelope is imprinted
with a picture of a crumpled envelope. Faux fractal refuse removed
      from

a wastebasket and smoothed to be used again, as if for a love that's
      always running
toward an abrupt end.


It's worse than my last thought, only your signature is still visible
      below
gray clouds. What was it you were telling me? That only four
      *hibiscus clayi* trees
are still alive on the slopes of the Nounou Mountains?
That the last p'ouli spent four years in a cage deep in tropical forest
      singing
for a mate that never came then died of West Nile Virus? I fold my
      letter, slip
it into the envelope to be postmarked years ago.

# Letter

Vasilina Orlova

While he was writing an old-fashioned letter
He noticed that the closer to the end he was
The stranger were things happening at the beginning
Of the page—it withered, twisted, curled, and finally a city
Was burning on the horizon
Black chains of smoke enclosed the sky
And when he'd finished his letter
The beginning was a trace of soot
Dispersed on the table.

# All Day She Wrote
### Lauren Camp

All day she wrote fragrant notes sticky as caramel.
Even as she slept, she did not resist the idle thrumming
of red words. She dreamt slowly and woke
twisted in sheets of flat afternoon sun. Her truth
was bruised. She knew the nature of things,
that his lungs were almost always wet with the slow
tapestry of gin, pulsing dots of liquid woven
into each repeated glass. She watched herself move
in a spiral, her insides round and mirrored as
what she had managed to reflect. She talked to others,
even laughed, ignored the gluey resin that collected
like sap between her legs. It wouldn't do to mention it.

He was headed someplace whole and specific
but he had limited storage space for the reasons why
he'd never get there. The distance between them
had grown into a grid of panic. She whispered to god
and the ceiling about strength, then said *yes*
when he returned. The answer stretched like spandex
until her flesh became elastic with its foolish shadows.
He trailed his hand lightly over the moss of her body,
tattooing her with need. She climbed over
into betrayal, held herself from her brief rejoicing.

# Letter to Baghdad

Lauren Camp


Even if my father never speaks a word of it, I will know
he brought a candle, a cough and the occupied side of his heart.
I will know the trees held him, that they rose above rooflines,
and where they met, he climbed and saw roads paved only with
      praises.
The sun he shouldered across oceans turned copper at his window.
I saw it too, on the grey edge of my childhood,
and I was marked when each day awoke. He devoured the silence,
the parts that could not be cured, and when he was hungry for it,
I swallowed that silence, his self-portrait of confession.
When I found an old shawl and silver teapot in the oven,
and he pretended he didn't know what they meant,
I remembered bitter lemons had moistened his mouth.
What he inhaled from his copious memory
left his tongue empty then full, and somehow I know
his tongue will always be brushed with the leaving.

One day we were talking about beginnings, and I had begun.
I wasn't at the center anymore, and we kept letting in a little air,
and he showed me a word for the boy he once was
and he showed me this Arabic word and in this way I knew
this was the most authentic mourning I would ever see.
And I saw it and he said it again,
and we were covered with it. Entirely covered. This was his home,
he said, as he gave me the address, the place
where the first time and the spurned and the color
and the milkmaid stood in the alley. And even though he didn't
      tell me
about yesterday and the day and the day and I never saw
any other way to tell it I never saw
heaven or the land that was black, one day I knew enough
to take the word from him and sip
every little thing every steeped thing

13

and there were many trees and not enough cold and we sat
by the river that curves in every direction and our hearts
lifted up to the birds.

# To the Captain of the Pequod
### Susan Rooke

My Husband,
I must tell you that each night
in sleep I hunt the sea for you,
from the safety of my bed
scanning the billowed down for
a man I regret to say I would
no longer know awake, so long have I
been forced to live without you.
By now I dream your hair salt-white
as the belly of your monster,
your face scored like the crests
and troughs of the endless waves

bearing you away. I daresay
you are rough and weather-stained
as the hull of your mistress-ship.
I pray your missing limb
no longer troubles you. I have
received your letters, but
with miles and months between.
Lacking news, I must invent my own.
Thus, evenings, once your son
is safe abed and dusk gutters, dying,
this candle lights my way

across your insufficient pages, until
at last I sleep in distant latitudes,
searching the haze on the horizon,
certain that one night I will spy you
as I toss upon this pillowed storm,
and catch a fleeting glimpse
of a proud white head breaching,
sounding, both nearer and farther
than I would like, as I rock

alone in the linen swells of my
landlocked, boundless ocean.

# Uncle Carroll's Letter from the Void
### Chip Dameron

None of you will ever know
which of us swam out first,
sputtering into the alien air,
giving up forever the gifts
of the womb for a tactile world
of uncertain hopes and certain death.
We were happiest floating
in our infinite universe,
neither hot nor cold, fingerlings
so fearless in our twinning.
You'd probably pick Charlie,
your father, Mr. Up at 5 A.M.,
Mr. Always Active and Organized,
as if he'd found his purpose
sooner than I had, as if he'd
pushed ahead to get the edge
on me, by those few minutes,
so when the flu finally found
our dusty oil town that fall
he'd be the toughened one,
the favored one who stayed on,
the only son that would matter.
How do you know I wasn't first,
the more curious one, risking
all comfort to cry my shock
out loud, telling Charlie just what
lay ahead, and he, ever cautious,
had held back as long as he could,
letting me suffer in my scrawny
lonely nakedness until he had
to face his future too. But neither
of us can tell you now, and so,
if you should care, you'll have
to imagine which of us wanted

to be first, and why, and how
that's shaped what you've become.

# Letter to Kyle in Michigan
### Gary Metras

Dear Kyle,
    Thank you for a copy of
your new book. It accompanied me
on my recent flight to Detroit, though
I had to change planes in Philadelphia
for some reason known only to the little
gods arguing then laughing in the top
floor offices of a US Airways tower
in a third city, the second one I had no
desire to have a fling with. I don't recall
packing your book, but when I opened
my briefcase after takeoff, there it was,
so forlorn beside my Kindle newly loaded
with that huge Brontës biography that will
be months and months, if not a year long.
(Yes, I do have that *fifty shades* book
also; and though I've been meaning to,
I haven't yet deleted it.) Forgive me
for spilling a few drops of coffee on
your page thirty-three when the airplane
went jittery a few moments ago.
I'm waiting for those droplets to dry
to discover whether Craig fell in love
with the shark or with the dark.
I think about the dark all the time now,
the way my parents are shrouded in it,
and one younger brother also, though
the still breathing one, the seething one,
has moved next door to the country
of dark; and I marvel at how both my
brothers-in-law opened that dark door
of health scares just this past winter
and slammed it shut before the dark
could settle into their lives. Kyle, I remember

your dark hair, darker eyes, darkest laugh,
yet I know that is a disguise, like how the iron
sky over Grand Rapids in winter masks warm
hearts. Forgive me, too, for writing this
on the empty pages at the back of your
new, inscribed to me book, now doubly
marred. My blank book was in my back-
pack in the overhead compartment
and I wanted to get these words on paper
right away before landing where they
would've evaporated the way in-cloud rain
never touches the ground, or how the quietness
inside the plane erupts into activity
when we land, and thought then becomes
impossible in that frenzy, so I wrote right
in your book. I hadn't planned on bringing
your book. It must have somehow known
Michigan is more home than Massachusetts.
They say certain books have an intelligence
all their own. Now I know what that means.

Much appreciated, Gary

# When the Envelope Opens, Open
### J. C. Todd

Comasia,
                    That morning above
Tetova and below the fretted
peaks of the Šar massif, our spirits
topsy-turvy, flushed clear by ozone
and early snow, we looked back
down the cirque to the city, a dollop
in the white-pocked valley held in place
by minarets, and saw how firmly
we are pinned by the bulk of flesh.
                                        What
is the root of such language in me,
etymology so personal
it sprouts from my cells?
                            A volume, thick,
on a scarred tabletop, acid-orange
light of late afternoon in a mill
town glazing the page. Pittsburgh. It's me
reading in the nave, hair held back by
a babushka like I saw in *Vogue.*
Oxblood loafers, madras skirt, circle
pin. It must be *Purgatorio,*
Dante's distinction between the flesh
of earthly attachment and the body
through which absolution is obtained.
The tongue, he is saying, is flesh, but
language is body, images lodged
in the seedbeds of cells, dormant
until miraculous bloom.
                        So what
if I have no Italian and you
have unstable English? Our emails
crosswrite, we read between the lines, pass

over to each other, not in words
but in that snowtop flare of greeting—

friend to friend. Wind tore what you said,
I half-heard. Our speaking—how garbled.
Transported in it, our language—pure.

# Letter from the Motherland
### Katia Mitova

My Faraway Daughter,

A good thing you've decided to write the story of your life
and to start with your first winter. What was it like?
you ask.
       I remember
I'd wake up at five and stare at the nightlight. I'd study
the mist of my breath, feel the formidable cold
of the stove.
Not a stove – a block of black ice that has invaded us
through the chimney, an informer, ensconced in a dark
overcoat, writing down the colors of dreams.
A stove so like the stocky man who took away your father
for owning a degenerate capitalist record:
Elvis' Christmas Album.
This happened on a strangely warm day, like spring:
December 13, 1957.
Then temperatures dropped by 60 degrees.
       Cloaked in a blanket, I would
                    descend to the basement.
Back with a bucket of coal. I'd feed the stove.
But the matches would break. Some would just smoke
without flame.
Finally, the damp, unread newspaper caught fire.
The splinters screamed but didn't wake you up.
       Only when the fire began to hum
your gray eyes opened huge
to the stove's red riot, its round lid jumping up.
I'd extract you from Grannie's embroidered coverlets
warm and wet. The day began
with your tiny, sharp fingernails on my swollen breast.
The robust certainty of your lips: you will not starve.
Your bottom—washed, dried, talcumed, kissed
almost sitting on a cloth nappy warmed by the stove.

Your toothless grin. My vow to spare you
true stories, false friends, and the wearing of black.
      As the day unbundled its face
          I'd go about my chores
thinking up answers to the questions
you'll start asking soon
             after you eat from another tree.
      Will write again.

Love,

Mom

# Letter to My Father
### Glen Sorestad

I don't know why I'm writing this letter—
you have been dead now for so long.
I haven't written you in fifty-four years
and though I haven't, I suppose I might
have done so, even one not meant to be
delivered. Had I written one a year
and filed each away in a folder somewhere,
it would serve as a reminder of all those
unanswered letters you wrote as a father
who cared enough to share his final years
with a son too busy finding his own way
to want or ever to seek a father's wisdom.
I may not even finish this letter.
It feels belated and unnecessary,
an apology for things undone,
all the omissions. A life measured in letters
written and sent, or letters unwritten,
contents like a wound. Tomorrow,
perhaps I'll start another.

# At the Ruins of the Roman Camp
### Sarah Webb

granaries, aqueducts
broken grave slabs

at one temple:
*to the nymphs of this place,*
*I have fulfilled my vow*

leather shoes
remains of a POW camp—
1000's of wooden huts

and, on parchment, linen, folded leaves of wood—
letters

a woman writes condolences
to one who has lost her child

a schoolboy's copying is corrected as sloppy

*We hope the underwear and socks will keep you warm*

*You are invited to the birthday celebration*

*I don't care what you say I owe—*
*no, I am not going to quit the garrison or the club!*

*Vindolanda, Scotland* 2001

# Dear Famous Female Singer

### Marian O'Brien Paul

I doubt you know I'm your mother-in-law-in-spirit. Impossible you could recall the wedding or recognize the groom, my son. For me to ask after the grandchildren you two have given me would be foolish. I know more about them than you do. Nor will I offer you condolences for the death of your infant. You needn't mourn. My son weeps enough real tears for you both.

You cannot be aware of your absent husband's schizo-affective disorder— nomenclature to classify his hallucinations and swings between depression and grand delusions. Do not be afraid. My son is not a Hinckley. He will not stalk you; he will not try to assassinate a public figure to attract your attention. Quite the contrary, if you knew your in-spirit-spouse, you would be comforted. He is fundamentally kind. Let me clarify.

Hallucinations skew perception: imagine biting into a plump apple but you find your teeth incising someone's arm. Would you relish the sensation or rue inflicting pain? How far would you go to avoid hurting someone you didn't know? *How far would you go?* Would you choose starvation? My overweight son erases himself to a skeletal frame, protecting this phantom
person.

He firmly believes he has married you in-spirit. I know he will never marry, never have a wife to love, children to cherish. He shows me the gifts he has collected to please you – a pillow he fringed during sessions in occupational therapy, perfume he won at bingo, a container packed with twenty years worth of pennies, each one he

27

believes God made priceless. I understand the depth of his loneliness, the edge of his despair.

I write you this letter to let you know how much you are loved, how lucky you are not to have my heartaches.

Sincerely,
Your Mother-in-Law-in-Spirit

# Dear Family, Read this First
### Donna Bowling

Nestled among the wills and powers of attorney
lies one self-adhesive, security-lined,
white envelope. Such a utilitarian vessel
to carry a lifetime of love and regrets.

Ever ready to have the last word,
I penned this missive to my sons,
just in case their father and I
failed to return from the mission trip.

As if I could speak to them from beyond,
to tell them I regret I have not been
a better parent. And how their existence
is the legacy that matters the most.

Funny I assumed their dad would die with me.
That we would cross the finish line
together and bring to an end
those conversations I never expected:

the ones that begin, "If I die first…"
In any case, how could I possibly
express the love and regrets
that stretch back almost half a century.

How could I say all the things I now know
that I could not have imagined
the night we married, so young, so hopeful,
those hard lessons we have learned together?

One envelope cannot contain
the love that has nourished
and bruised and comforted,
and thrilled and shaped me.

No, I'll leave these brief instructions,
one more reminder of the love I have lived with them.

# Postcards from Alaska
### Jerry Bradley

Consider what this time shall mean
to inland seas that bleed nightmare,
to rookeries blanched with oil-bathed birds
and clutches of greasy seals pupped on shore.

A childhood friend unfit to save
sends the postcard of a predator
from his near-glacier home. "Don't spare
this trench for anything better,"

he writes; "the sky turns to winter
here too. Spend it while you can, pal,
and forget how you think it was.
Sink your thing into a hot gal."

He signs each one "Alaskan love
and cold pussy"—he always has—
and shames me like warm thoughts of home.
I pretend I can live without the gas.

# Dear Neighbor
### Jerry Bradley

We have spoken about the fire ants, and I hope
I am forgiven. You gave me something to think about,
and now and again, like today, I do. So let's let the old days
be done if only because spring is here at last and it is once again
the time of seed. We've both made another circle around the sun,
and soon the sticky tongue of summer will be on us all. I will try
to heed the maxim to *love my neighbor as myself*, although life
        has taught
me that love can be a fine servant but is often a tyrannical master.

I know we had words, Pete, but I didn't get to use all of mine.
I did not complain about the four turkeys you fattened last Thanksgiving,
how they found their way over the fence to my patio
where they stared at their reflections in the sliding door
every afternoon for a month, defecating incessantly.
Nor did I fault your leaving the driveway floodlights on all winter,
though their brightness sneaked past my bedroom curtains, because, well,
it is a rough neighborhood and somebody should leave them on.
And I know, I know my cats frequented your pansy bed far too often,
but did that really warrant your adopting Cerberus from the no-kill
        shelter?

Well, if my cats can modify their behavior, so can I, I guess. All we need
to know about life is that the liver is a regenerative organ,
but the heart is not. That's an idea we both should raise a glass to.
Today we have only the sun, but later the sky will be full of stars,
and next year we will both fall to our knees dreaming tomatoes.

So what I ask for tonight is this: when it's dark and far Arcturus beckons,
please pen your dog and douse your light. My long chair,
that yearly facsimile of hope, is already out and waiting,
and, when I'm home, I hope it, the darkness, and a tall glass
will be able to work their magic. I ask you, for once let me be
the gutshot cat who upon returning home gets the comfy chair.

# Winterhilfswerk
# Des Deutschen Volkes
France, 6 Jan. '45
  Sherry Craven

"Dear Sherry: I hope you never have to see villages
shelled in half, blown up" the yellowed letter begins,
having traveled through shattered war zones and murky decades,

delivered sixty years after the ink dried, a six-cent stamp
crowning the right top corner of an envelope looking like
a flag with red and blue stripes all around the edges—air mail.

A colonel, his orderly, two guards and his driver wrapped
into the lives of a French family in Nazi-occupied France,
winter days enfolded into pickles, hot water, patched clothes,
warmth, refuge served with occasional home-baked cherry pie.

A country bound by evil, surrounded by tight, invisible lines,
days bound by restrictions, nights falling on the family like a shroud.
He writes, "No children have gloves for their poor little hands

and no warm clothes like you have, and their faces are very red."

I hold a warm cup of Starbucks and stare at the fragile letter
sending me a war-torn life when strangers found a holiness,

some refuge in one another, embraced by a house "shelled,
half blown away." The letter carries killings, bombings,
hunger, freezing cold, tattered soldiers, a family

pulling their days through their stone-cold fear, their barbed wire
        fence
of a life to a gratitude warm as their scant fireplace arrive at my
        door.

The brown-edged envelope delivers a rock pile of words heavy,
    tumbled.

Carried within the space of a 2 X 6 yellowed envelope, addressed in a
    fragile,
blue-penned scrawl are the visceral words, the music of French
    voices,
the pain of frozen fingertips, the genesis of living and dying
    handwritten in faded ink.

# To My Sons
### Sherry Craven

Well, I guess you're not boys now, grey hair
peeks through the years along your collar,
around your ears. Can this be?

Chunky, musky little boys run through my head,
plastic scooters make crazy trails around my heart,
and at night in dreams, I reach into deep water to pull you to me.

But still, actuality offers me pen and paper, whispers
instructions like a second grade teacher, "Write,
and stay on the line, out of the margins."

So this letter is to be filed with my will; I hope the words will
somehow float to you like leaves drift on October breezes. I have
been worrying about such things as the rosewood desk, the Haviland
china, much less the antique silver.

I envision the two of you overwhelmed by my long-gathered
possessions, grabbing a beer to stave off multi-colored frustrations,
missing me and mourning, yet all the while knowing your kids' soccer
practice is at five and your wives want you home,

so I reach into the shoe box of memories in my head
and decide to let go the desk. I am writing this letter to
tell you that what I really want to leave to you is the sunset I saw
from the patio last week carving trees limbs into the sky.

Also, I want to trap in a fruit jar all the fireflies of happy, joy,
kindness and hand to you, to keep forever by your bed.

There is a particular rose out front I saw this morning and a song
I loved once and, oh yes, the violin concerto. I want to give these to you
and I suppose most of all, I want to take all the forgiveness I have
        been given

throughout the years, wrapped in various shades of people and be sure you have such mercies close by combined with bits and fragments of love—you should be okay.

My attorney thinks me crazy, but this is what I earnestly bequeath to you both in hope you will pass along my letter with some added PS's of your own.

This letter then, is my codicil.

Love,

Your Mother

# Who is Writing? Wodwo Two
### Kornelijus Platelis

Who is writing? Nosing here, turning sheets over
Following the faint stain on the air to the table's edge
I look at the mirror. Who am I to split
The glassy gleams looking upward I see the top
Of the table above me upside down very clear
What I am doing here in the mid-air? Why do I find
this language so interesting as I inspect most secret
interior and make it my own? Do these papyri weeds
know me and name me to each other have they
seen me before, do I fit in their world? I seem
separate from the ground and not rooted but dropped
out of nothing casually I've no threads
fastening me to anything writing I can go anywhere
I seem to have been given the freedom
of this place who writes then? And picking
words off this language stump gives me
no pleasure and it's no use so why do I do it
me and doing that coincided very queerly
But what shall I be called to sign am I the first
have I a teacher what style do I use what
shape am I am I huge if I go
to the end of this way past these books past these trees
till I get tired that's touching one wall of me
for the moment if I sit still how everything
stops to read me I suppose I am the exact center
but there's all this what is it roots
roots roots roots and here's the paper and who
is writing – you, ted, even if dead, or me?

# A Letter Addressed to a Man with a Remarkable Future

Mark Podesta

I opened up the envelope
And I was swallowed whole
And what I saw was a world not of my own
With an egg yolk light and a periwinkle floral sky
There was a running silver river that looked like ice cubes floated
      in it
And a pristine forest a shade of green so fluorescently natural
      that it looked fake
And on the bank of the river was a home
With white panel siding and a red door
Inside there was a fabulously translucent hiddenness that made
      the house charming
And there was an uproarious much to do about nothing that settled
      in the kitchen
(The backspace key is broken for some nameless reason to me)
Golden lamp bulbs were reflected on to the ceilings
With a loose sink wave that flooded the hallway
A crazy rapturous melancholic frenetic splurge of a record was being
      played
A record that just about every almost anybody turn of the century
would have heard already
"But that may seem to play problematic!"
Said the man with the sardine mustache
"Hear me
Hear me
I am a broken bell that does not stir save for when I hear that
      justice has been served
Ah don't you see this is a world unjointed
From another space and another time
True man can fly and sing but you people are stuck here
We are the possibility of another future
Had his mind had another impulse

Had there been another psychological possibility then there
        would have been a lot of rapid change
But seeing as he picked the one he has
We are now stuck here
Nothing will change here
Do you understand this?
We are running on your random access memory bank and
        reference chart
Looking to walk a premeditated path
That may have actually been intentional
And that unsettles you
Freaks you out if you will"
Someone down the hall lectured philosophy and water
He was constructing a conversation about his world that was so
        volatile
"Combustible futures and brightly painted windows
Hooplah
Hooplah
Please leave now kindly"
But now he was in a whirlwind fit of inexhaustible manic
        excitement that flared and roared because we may have
        been discussing the validity of Ginsberg
And I maybe just maybe had said something along the lines of
        this,
"There's a reason he is canon material and that reason is that the
        entire piece itself symbolizes something on a separate
        plane from the lateral meaning.
Outside of the view of the poetry and the poem itself
That is incredible in and of itself"
But anyway I must cease the digressions of knowledge
Next, I found myself outside the house and no longer debating
I was among a crowd of otters and they were all walking in a
        unanimous line and everything looked so sloppy but
        uniform
So animalistic yet tame
There were swords raining from the sky when I began to enter
        the castle

at the mouth of the river that read "Royal House of
Depravation"
It was a violent storm but we stayed dry and alive inside castle
I was trying to find my way out but I was lost and the light at the
  top of the sky was starting to look like the sun, no longer
  the mouth of the envelope
Then I thought
What if I stayed here?
What if I stayed in the house?
And watched my parents grow old
And worked at the coffee shop down the river
And was content
And drank a casual drink in the backyard around the water
  in the summer time
And I found a girl who I just thought had the most ravishingly
  beautiful dress on
And it shined in the light
And every time I saw her I saw that dress not her
And we had kids
And I kept my shit together
And the kids carried my name
Because that's what children do
And I grew old
And so did they
And I would spend my days looking out of my window with my
  dog
And the room I was in was dark and menacing but the window
  was bright and promising
And this little house would shrink
And this little world would stale
And this little existence would cry—
I CANNOT STAY—
The sky got dark
And the rumblings of thunder came from the belly of the world
The mountains rose
The rivers raced
The wind spun and trees flew

In no time the house on the river was in the sky
Losing its shudders and throwing its red door
I reached up to the small light and by some work of a miracle my
        arm reached the opening in the sky
I flew threw clouds thick with rain and my body kept soaring
Lightning scratched at me
And booms of thunder rang enough to make my ears bleed
Pieces of the house flew at me
And the sun disappeared
But I reached the opening
My arm clasped on to its side
And I hoisted myself up
I pulled my body over the opening's threshold
Then I was hanging on the hole with my waist on the cusp
And I wiggled my way up
My head in my world
And my feet in the dead one
Then I began to push myself and eventually kicked my feet around
        mercilessly and wiggled free
But before I left I must say I did spend some time in that world
Because it was pleasant and sweet and planned
And I met someone
And they came to the house
And I fell in love
And he fucked me
Because I was a cheap fuck
Needing to be filled
And held
He was straight
But he did it anyway
Because he had a heart for me
A heart that I had thought was actually just pity
Like I was something to be pitied
And because he looked at me like I was such a pity
Like I was this lost child in a world of adult hustlers
But he fucked me
And the rawness of this fuck was sensational

But it was straight and rigid and felt like work
I was excited but somehow knew it wasn't the same for him
So I felt uncomfortable but I was accustomed to this uncomfort
And began to like it
And was pleasured by it
Because somewhere deep down inside of me I had this deeply
       wrong understanding of love and understanding
And I loved him but he loved me different
And I saw the world as this grand place of exploration and love
And he saw it as this dimly lit Popsicle box of forgotten feeling
       and fairytale fucks
He fucked me that night
And a couple nights more
And after every fuck he fell a little more in love with me
And I fell a little more out of love with him
And in the end I was just a cheap fuck
But also a Poet—
I CANNOT STAY—
I fell out of the envelope to the ground
And in a primordial mess of water and mass I was curled on the
       ground sopping wet and naked
Because I had lived a life
Because I had lived an experience
And now I finally felt like I had the chance to finally just
       simply—be
I was now new to this world
And now I wish that my parents hadn't been so perfect
That they challenged me and made me frustrated
Because then maybe this inescapable hold that they have on me
       wouldn't be here
My soul is attached to them
Why should I leave if they are part of me
But I should have been told what to do
I should have been hollered at
Because that's something special
That would have given me authority to leave
That would have given me authority to prosper

That would have given me authority to live—
Thank you for the letter, Mother
I will write back soon
When I am done leaving.
I think I will begin my letter with "The calm envelops the storm."

# Chupacabra Finds an Envelope to Send His Love Letter

### Clarence Wolfshohl

It is a plain white, dime store
envelope you can see a check
through, one corner dented
as if it's been in a fender-bender
with a Fed-Ex package
at a country crossroads,

but it fits his new romantic need
to trace his heart in #2 lead
and in a squiggled alphabet.
He sniffs the air for goat
but finds only huisache blossoms
on the air, and the l's and e's
grow less stooped and gnarled
under his hand. He worries
over the closing: "all my love"
or "affectionately," not knowing which
goes better with his "my darling"
salutation. Goes with the first
and a row of x's and o's
like his burning red eyes.

He folds the ripped-edge spiral
notebook  sheet, stuffs it into
the envelope, licks the sweet glue
of the flap, sticks the forever stamp
onto his claw then the corner
opposite the dent, and stops, not knowing
to whom it should be addressed.

# Due Cultivation
## Clarence Wolfshohl

I key this note from the moraine
shoved and carried to this Missouri edge
from Canadian or Arctic earth
millennia ago. Up the shoreline
of a nearby lake is a perfectly round
stone, some three feet across,
scraped from Minnesota rock,
tumbled smooth and round
on its journey down
the slope of the continent.
It is in a clearing of hickory and oak,
the woods so dense that, but
in winter, you cannot see more
than a moment's walk into their heart.
And this density, this darkness,
is what one must comprehend
in the woods. It is the soil, the clay
so thick a potter dreams, good or bad,
its turning. It is the sky, the dark
silhouetted filigree of leaf and limb
that obscures the blue. It is the breath,
the huff and murmur of wind-inspired crowns,
each tree –sassafras or oak—
speaking its own ancient tongue.

And here on my nine acres
among rolling hills, shallow ponds,
and woodland, a few miles from the Missouri,
the wet mark of the glacier's end,
in these past thirty years I have
tended my garden as old Candide
advised, sometimes with yield,
sometimes without, but always, I hope,
with due cultivation.

# On Stationery of Light
### Larry D. Thomas

I can't remember the last time
I penned a letter to a friend, in cursive,
but I would never have thought
that my next correspondence
would be this: printed with the pressing
of square, black keys on stationery
of light. But here it is, long after
the passing of much too many years.

I've lived in the Great Chihuahuan Desert
for two and one-half years now, perusing
a sky so blue, so vast, and so clean,
even of a wisp or two of clouds,
I find myself probing its depths
as one would a tome of philosophy.

The wind, though, in its myriad forms
often preempts the sky as my preferred
subject of inquiry: wafting, soughing,
and howling like a crazed prophet
long devoid the encumbrances of flesh,
so saturate with sun, moon, starlight,
and the desultory triad of death,
the buzz of flies, and history, he can't stop
the unremitting oozing of his prophecies.

# Satori

*for Robert Jones*
Wally Swist

Yes, it has been long enough. It has been long enough that
      hearing
from you this evening is much like having stepped onto what is

apparently an unfamiliar subway car, and in a moment of the
      terrific
velocity of G-force, I find myself, years later, sitting at my
      worktable

here in my studio near the foot of Long Mountain in South
      Amherst,
Massachusetts, writing you. I especially appreciate your emailing

the photograph of you standing beside Robert Spiess, who is
      wearing
the medal from his having been presented with the Shiki Award,

and holding open the bound citation in his hands. You are
      correct
in your assessment that he was in league with Emerson and
      Mencken,

as an editor. Anyone can see what the award meant to him by
his facial expression and body language. Did you know that he
      was

a surrogate father to me?  Thank you for the update on your
      Lavelle
translations—I appreciate that. Louis Lavelle being the Christian

mystic of the *intelligentsia,* in direct opposition to Sartre's
　　　existentialism.
*The Act of Presence* is a text I look forward to rereading. Could it
　　　be that

I remember studying Lavelle all those years ago? I feel that
　　　through
you, the universe touched me on the shoulder this evening, and I
　　　am

grateful that you precipitated my own *presence* in a deeply-
　　　experienced
*satorial* flash—just in an instant. D. T. Suzuki wrote: *Satori is
　　　the raison*

*d'être of Zen, without which Zen is no Zen.* You reminded me of
　　　the truth
of who I am, where my eternal home is, here or elsewhere: *in the
　　　moment.*

# Shopping List:  A Stolen Poem
### Judith Toler

Dear Lady:

You lost your list at Albertson's.
I found it at the check-out counter
where, after signing for my Mastercard,
I couldn't resist.  it was your spidery
black handwriting—too tempting.
So I stole your words.

I mean, what was I supposed to do—
turn them in to Lost and Found, advertise
in the Personals column, Lost Connections?
Besides, you were the careless one,
the one who left your list, mysterious
as the buzzings of a fly.

Thirteen lines in three stanzas—
spare and strange and not at all like
the artichokes and oysters, pomegranates,
shampoos and scented lotions in my cart:

    *silver polish*

    *Slim fast*

How chaste you are.

    *milk*
    *crackers*

My grandma used to call it graveyard stew.

    *fruit*

Just fruit, no particular kind.
Your other items were not anything to eat


    *dust pan*
    *Ivory snow*

and yes, after the first small stanza break:

    *ice blue losenges*

You misspelled lozenges
but I love the ice blue part.


So far, only eight lines.  See, already
I'm beginning to forget your words written
on narrow shiny paper that looks like tape
for an adding machine.

Oh yes, quickly three more lines:

    *note paper*
    *stamps*
    *envelopes*

And then the final space, the long drop
between the second stanza and the last,
the long white drop:


    *razor*
    *black thread*

# The River-Merchant's Wife:  Her Last Letter
## *After Li Po/Ezra Pound*
### Judith Toler

The golden leaves fell early this autumn
and cold has silenced the crickets.
Your mother won't stop weeping, grows angry
when she looks at my flat belly, makes me sweep
over and over again the empty corners.
No tea I ever make is sweet enough for her mouth.

Three times a day I climb the watch-tower
searching for you, though boats are few this time of year
and winter winds pull at my clothes.
I shiver, longing to stay warm by the fire,
but when the messenger arrives from far Ku-to-Yen,
I wrap myself tight in robes, gather some
small things for the long journey to meet you.

On the road, the cherry blossoms burst into pink clouds,
bloom then fade and fall too quickly to the ground.
I want to paste them back onto the branches.

At seventeen I reach the swirling waters of Chu-tang.
I am tired and lie down on soft grass by the shore,
watch for you among the river dolphins
while high above us, at the rim of the steep gorge
temple bells ring and monkeys make sounds
like cries from heaven.

Through the shallows, I carry to you, My Lord, this letter,
your bamboo flute, two tiny cups to hold plum wine,
tea leaves, a few grains of rice in an earthen bowl,
straw from the mat that was our bed.

The swirling water loosens my hair.

From the sleeves of my white robe spill offerings
to the dragons of the river Kiang—
cowrie shells and sweets, a lotus blossom, blue pebbles—
prayers that the river spirits take pity on us
and kindly monks sail little lanterns on the waves
to light our way to shore,

for I have traveled farther than Cho-fu-Sa to meet you.
I have traveled below the silver belly of the moon.

# To Hypnos, God of Sleep
Jeanie Greensfelder

You creep into my bed,
envelop me,
erase my worries,
and together
we dream.

But on those nights
when you don't show,
and I know you're out
sleeping with others,
I wait and watch and
add you to my worries.

You ruin my nights,
disturb my days,
and you never listen.

My counselor says,
*You're stuck with him.*
*Calm him with chamomile,*
*soothe him with love talk.*

That night you watch
as I brew tea,
bathe, dab lavender,
turn on Brahms,
and get into bed early,
hoping you're pleased,
hoping you stay the night.

# Living with Art
## Barbara Daniels

Dear Anthony LaBriola,
My hand went out to the book you left
in Room 301 and it was mine. I took
what I wanted the way I stole a man once,
        a boy really, told myself
it didn't matter, then cried in his bathtub
with claws. Anthony, you've gone to Florida
with your girlfriend, and *Living with Art*
was too big to fit in the car
with your summer clothes,
        sleeping bags, iPads.
The week I stole your book
my mother asked which was better,
a lumpectomy or a mastectomy.
        It's about the first thing
she's ever asked me, and I'm 64.
I could see she was leaning
toward the mastectomy
so I said, "Go for it.
Have them take the whole thing."
Why mess around, right, Anthony?
        She has a prosthesis now.
Every night she washes it
in liquid Ivory and puts it
in its little cradle
so the oils of her body
        don't eat away at it
before two years are up
and the insurance people
give her another one.

That's what I call living with art,
the prosthesis in its cradle
        like the shape of a child

in the sculptured arms of its mother,
        so smooth I want to touch it,
but when I do, it is cold.

# For Friends Who Send Poems
### Mark Vinz

In with the blare of circulars,
tidy notices in anonymous envelopes,
lurid promises of fortunes to be won,
there is a small package with my name on it,
light seeping from tears in the wrapping.
For a moment, everything stops:
I turn a book of poems over in my hands,
fingering the sheen of the cover,
the curve of each letter.
I see a face beside a window, expectant,
looking up with the thinnest smile,
and at that moment I remember
just how unfaithful I am:
I will abandon each page that
calls me to one of my own;
it may take years before I finish reading.
Then I see another face by the window,
my face, and I know again
that what we give, we get back,
what we lose, someone else will find for us,
and what is sent out will stay
beyond all finishing and forgetting.

# The Hold
### Charles Douthat

There it is! Just before putting out the light.
Here in the doorway to his room.
The unmistakable smell of him
though his train pulled out an hour ago.
Not a child's smell anymore, but a young man's air
of college nights and long wool coats
and jokes so cool they cannot be explained.
*You had to be there, Dad,* he says.

Now in his scented wake I wait,
knowing he'll soon be gone for good,
graduating to some new city,
paying too much rent.
And this room where for years he slept
and read, while brown hair broke through
on his face and chest... Soon
it will be a place for someone else to rest.
But not quite yet.

This fragrant air is sweet to me
tonight. The dusty heat rising
from baseboard vents. The windows tight.
His house-warmed high school books
upright in their case.
Like me, they've done their work.
What we instructors had to say
has all been said. And what he took to heart
is as unfathomable now
as what he cast away.

For he's moving on and on his own
to worlds he'll live to see
but I will never fully know. Of course
he'll stop again to sleep and eat.

We'll speak again of Charlemagne
and Russell Crowe.  But the being of him,
that second self housed for years
nearly inside my skin, is elsewhere,
flowing on, flown.

How does a father live, I wonder.
But it's late now. At the stair
my wife is calling. And so I remember
that morning my son was first handed to me,
still blood-smudged and birth-slippery.
And because I was a new father then
and because my inexperience showed
the midwife taught me how to hold a child properly.
*Lightly now,* she cautioned.
But also pulling at my arms, testing me,
until I sensed what it meant
not to let go.

# Sunday Morning, Hardly Hearing the News, Looking Elsewhere, Noticing
### Dana Heifetz

envy
lopes
sent
from
treacherous
eyes

to stamp you

       post *that*!

# Mailing a Letter

David Breeden

One envelop from
a lighted slot—a
quarter, was it?—
stamped, ready
from a clicking
machine. What

was the stuff
the handle was
made of that I
pulled on that
night, wishing
for gloves? The

screech of rusted
metal in the wall.
One letter off—
what could have
been so urgent?—
out into the dark.

# Post (fall) Marks
### Alan Berecka

To seal the envelope
the tongue risks
the sharp edge
and licks the glue.

Risks the worse cuts—
paper cuts—
paper cuts burning
in the taste of glue.

So much risked
to hide our naked
thoughts from the bearer—
the reader of addresses

who still takes
every Sunday off.

# (Go, sad letter)
### Bill Sullivan

Go, sad letter.
Let the world know that once I
laughed and played in the Thai
fields and shyly eyed my first
love, Yuan, on my thirteenth birthday.

By the times the rains had ceased
and the rice had been harvested,
we had shared stories, sang songs,
and dreamt of the cloudless days ahead.

Let them know that the sun disappeared
when the Bangkok broker came to appraise
the young girls of my village. I rue
the day he cast his greedy eyes on me.
To my penniless father he offered a way
to pay his bills; to me a new life in the city
where I would find a rewarding career.

Let your readers know I was not deceived.
When my father counted the broker's loan,
and I heard the agent say my work would pay
off the debt, my heart splintered and a woeful wind
swept the pieces away. When I left with the broker,
I could not look at my father for one reason.
And I could not look at Yuan for another.

Sad letter, let all the too young- to- be women
In Thailand, Cambodia, the Ukraine, Turkey
Hungary, Columbia and America know
that there is no glamorous city awaiting them.
Explain that only pain, abuse and imprisonment
reside there. Tell them that in this and other
carnal houses we are forged and hammered

into sex slaves, sex machines, forced day and night
to pollute our bodies, to hollow out our souls,
until we are of no worth to anyone,
not our parents, not our suitors, not the villagers,
not the urban dwellers. They will turn their heads;
say we are unclean, unredeemed, unwanted.

But before you close, become an angry letter.
Scald with boiling words the shameless men
who come sneaking  through these doors
doing to us what they would not do to their
daughters or sisters. Out the corrupt authorities
who close their eyes as they collect their bribes.
As for the perpetrators, demand that they be paraded
through the streets and then sentenced to wander
under the distant desert's blistering sun where
they can begin their life-long  penance.

When you do this, I shall sign my name.

# II. Received

# Envelope from a Leap Year
### Katia Mitova

I open the wax-sealed envelope: a day of summer toward the end
      of a long winter.

Father and I on a yellow tandem. We pedal quickly but are not
      moving. I like this.

My brother in the garden, still a baby, crawling toward a blue-green
      caterpillar, never reaching it.

A tawny puppy perpetually chasing its tail.

My mother on the porch, at her sewing machine, hemming
      a length of white cotton without a thread, without making
      any noise.

We are happy. Suddenly a bee buzz. Am I the only one who hears?

I jump off the bike and follow the sound to the window
      of my room, which
is all iced save for a small peephole scratched by the bee. Inside,
      winter continues.

I step back, slowly fold the day, put it back in the envelope
moisten the glue on the flap with my tongue
and seal Being & Becoming together.

# Delivery
### Cindy Wolfe Boynton

The first real proof of my existence
arrived by mail on a Friday, the envelope almost
as blank as me, my name handwritten in tight
blue script like grandma's Christmas card list,

Crinkled, coffee-splotched
pages of aunts cousins nephews in-laws:
family who really weren't mine at all,

All listed in functional columns
like the story of my beginning
that now might not always need
a once upon a time.

| Mother | Father |
|---|---|
| Blonde | Redhead |
| Episcopalian | Lutheran |
| 5'7 | 5'9 |
| Her studying to teach | |
| Him pursuing physics | |
| Both 20, fair, green-eyed | |

Nineteen words of nothing but everything.
Deliverance on agency letterhead.
Finally a start. A truth. Me.

# Sealed with Moonlight

Kyle Anderson

I snake through West Texas,
      my shadow a horse
            toting saddlebags
where I keep your letter,
      a sack of spider eggs
            in a Mason jar, & bolas.

A jackrabbit jumps,
      I trip it, lift a rock,
            its eye throws blood
like cactus spines.
      Chameleons on a stone
            Observe, charring clouds.

Before the fire
      I stuff your letter
            down the rabbit's gullet,
jar some rising smoke,
      eat roasted words, the meat,
            Then watch the spiders slow

Within the glass
      Like a sustained note
            on a guitar string. I lick
blood from my fingers,
      twist open the jar
            beneath me, the smoke

Clings to my face
      like your caramel body,
            the first time I felt into you—
A coyote rib thrust inside
      a cactus where I knelt,
            gulping the harbored rain.

# I Should Be Eating Cake in the Frick with Rembrandt

Vivian Shipley

It's my birthday; I'm sealed in, no E-vite but an enveloped
invitation. Wings beating black, even with an insatiable appetite
for bluefish, a cormorant is shocked into Connecticut sky
by a jet roaring over Morgan Point out of New Haven. No one
is coming to fly me in, fly me out. Who cares if I recycle?

Summer's slouching to an end; I should do just one thing
right here, right now but I would rather grind memories.
Why can't I be Rembrandt painting his 1658 *Self Portrait*?
Last spring in the Oval Room, if Frick's guard had turned
his head, I could have caressed rugged brush strokes of

Rembrandt's aging flesh. His knees almost missing, I could
have ended up on his lap. Mercedes-Benz habits, bankrupt
at 52, his art hawked, his home lost, his cane is still silver
tipped, he is draped in fur. Floppy black velvet hat as crown,
painter's stick as scepter, he is potentate of his studio.

Probably because like me he is overweight, a wine red
sash is belted high on a golden-yellow jerkin making him
look busty, maternal. Unlike poets, Dutch painters did not
use self-portraiture for personal probing—but still I wonder
if Rembrandt was thinking what his talent was worth?

Maybe he, too, was not much good to himself any longer.
Pink chafe mark on his chin, Rembrandt shadowed his eyes,
spot of white on one ignites drama that smolders within.
*Self Portrait* could be a tag sale with splashy strokes, chunky
surfaces: outsider, visionary who is shunned, painting only

for himself. I'd have advised him to master ignoring mirrors,
move everything as I have done out of the medicine cabinet,

strip walls bare of any glass that dares to reflect a face I don't
recognize, a body I want to elongate. Painted with a splotched
hand, ravenous as a cormorant for fame, how could Rembrandt

have doubted his genius? Perfectly lit, wrinkles in both cheeks
have deepened to creases. For me light's the thief, not a friend.
If only I could muster his courage, stare into a mirror, maybe
the head reflected wouldn't be a gray mastodon. No Rembrandt,
still, I am in no rush to leave my body—not just yet.

# Upon Receiving a Letter
### Vivian Shipley

With my yo-yo, I walk the dog and go clear around
the world, but otherwise, I stand still, look at weed

and bramble. Slitting the envelope, I read that my friend
is taking off for Europe Tuesday, a look at Wimbledon,

a Scandinavian cruise before she begins to study
at Oxford. Her daughters will travel with boyfriends

from Paris to Rome and then explore Italy on their own.
She'll join them for a long weekend in Geneva, then

back to England for a theater course. Imagine, six hours
of credit for going to plays in London with Roger Reese,

Derek Jacobi and Ben Kingsley! Oh yes, her lecture
at the Folger in Washington went well. It was elegant—

an occasion—one of many she has been allowed to enjoy.
I haven't been anywhere yet, but it's on my list: *let's get*

*this act on the road; shake a leg; let's get cracking; I'm*
*clearing out of here.* If I go too fast, I won't see anything.

If I slow down, I won't be here to see everything before
it disappears as the horizon does, a line like black spots

by the sides of my eyes. Turn full faced, they're gone.
At a mosque in Damietta, there is a column of pumice.

If I lick it until my tongue bleeds, it must bleed, I will be
cured of restlessness. Such choices: spots like my friend's

letter that suck at my eyes or tongues that must bleed. It is
easier to stay put, leave the mail unopened, than to plead:

take me along like floss for your teeth or bifocals you
never wear. I'll be light, no more weight than a paper sack.

Fading like pink liliums, no ardor carries me through July;
everything holds its position: poems, a chair, typewriter

without a ribbon. Perhaps if I could afford to stay on
in Dover when hotels are shutting, umbrellas are folded,

I would decide not to join my friend in London or Paris,
but sit reading in the library next to *Maison Dieu*, or stand

by chalk cliffs that trace the coast. Listening for a gull's call,
waiting to watch light shining on the Strait, there would be

eighteen miles of English Channel for me to cross, opening
like years or the gulf lying between France, my friend and me.

# about time

### fragments of a correspondence between Anne Viscountess Conway (1631-1679) and Isaac Newton (1643-1727)

Steven Schroeder

1

*(marginal notes in Isaac Newton's hand, in a text later attributed to Anne Viscountess Conway)*

*god* is a word among words.
in other words,
*god* is

a concept by which we—

that is to say
we say *my*

*god* we
say

*god*
*of.* but

*deitas* is another
matter. i'll say it again

*god* is a concept
by which we
measure.

the thing is
*god* is
god

of. god is
substantially

one. all things
are contained in

god and
move.

but god does not act
on them nor they on him. all

eye, all ear, all
brain, all arm, all
sense, all act, not at all

human. we
have no
idea.

2

*(a fragment of a letter written by Anne Viscountess Conway to Isaac Newton shortly after his appointment as Lucasian Professor of Mathematics at Cambridge University)*

It is clear, sir, that you follow our esteemed teacher Henry More, to whom I defer in all matters of wit and understanding. But on this, I differ. For God's dwelling in space to take place, it is necessary that space make way; and it is the act of God's dwelling there then that moves it. Still, it moves.

3

*(from Newton's response, possibly a draft, probably undelivered)*

As I see it, sunlight is the same light as the light in a cooking fire, the same light as light reflected on earth and in the planets. To effects of the same kind the same cause should be attributed; and between the attribution of a cause and the observation of an effect we come to think we know what moves as well as what is moved. Still, we move.

4

*(a fragment of a letter written by Anne Viscountess Conway to the Lucasian Professor of Mathematics at Cambridge University)*

there is no time in god, no
change, no composition, no
division, no shadow

of turning. god (as you
say) is one

substantially. But I hold that god,
distinct, is, still, not
separate

from creatures. god is
present in every single one
most intimately

there is no
time in god, no
change, no knowledge,

no will, no
passion. god knows

nothing.

5

*(marginal note written by Isaac Newton in a text later attributed to Anne Viscountess Conway)*

I say, again, *god* is a concept by which we. Measure, beginning and end, where we are, in time.

6

*(a fragment of a letter written by Anne Viscountess Conway to the Lucasian Professor of Mathematics at Cambridge University)*

there is a word
in god, in essence


one and the same, the source
of god's knowing god
and god's knowing
every other
thing.

7

*(from Conway's journal, a reference to a letter she received from Newton via Henry More)*

Speaking of word, Mr. Newton says he suspects one must look to Euclid's *Elements* to hear it. A word of god, he writes, must, if it is nothing else, be measured.

8

*(a fragment of a letter written by Anne Viscountess Conway to the Lucasian Professor of Mathematics at Cambridge University)*

god made creatures with whom to speak,
but they did not take to light, so
god, all light, diminished

light to make space
where creatures could dwell,

space like an empty circle, space for worlds,
an actual place, the soul of the word
that filled the space.

soul united with light
to make a subject —
speaker, spoken.

9

*(from Conway's journal, a reference to a letter she received from
Newton via Henry More)*

Speaking of limits, Mr. Newton recalls that Euclid maintained
epiphanies, bounded by lines, have length and width alone...

10

*(a fragment of a letter written by Anne Viscountess Conway to the
Lucasian Professor of Mathematics at Cambridge University)*

there is no time
so small that it cannot be divided
into smaller times.

an infinite number of times,
a time that is infinitely divisible.
a being outside time

time is
nothing but
the motion of creatures.

no motion, no
time. no time, no

creatures. the nature
of every creature is
to be in motion.

11

*(marginal note written by Isaac Newton in a text later attributed to Anne Viscountess Conway)*

still, they move

12

*(a fragment of a letter written by Anne Viscountess Conway to the Lucasian Professor of Mathematics at Cambridge University)*

god cannot act without reason. though
a most free agent, god is also
most necessary.

as there is an infinity of times
there is an infinity
of worlds.

there is an infinity of creatures,
each containing an infinity in itself
on and on and on...

there are no spaces where god is not,
and in any space where god is

there must be creatures because
where god is, god does.

the action of god is one act, because
there can be no succession in god.

if a creature were reduced to its least parts
all motion and operation in creatures
would cease and it would be

as though the creature thus divided
were pure nothingness.

the division of things is never in terms of
the smallest mathematical term
but of the smallest physical term.

13

*(marginal note written by Isaac Newton in a text later attributed to Anne Viscountess Conway)*

A compilation of least things, ever closer approximation to the curve
a moving body traces over time.

14

*(a fragment of a letter written by Anne Viscountess Conway to the Lucasian Professor of Mathematics at Cambridge University)*

when matter is so divided
it disperses into physical monads,
such as it was in the first state of its formation,
then it is ready to resume its activity and become spirit.

a consideration of the infinite divisibility of everything
into always smaller parts is not an inane or useless theory,

but of the very greatest use for understanding the causes
and reasons of things and for understanding
how all creatures from the highest to the lowest
are inseparably united one to another by their subtler
mediating parts, which come between them and are emanations
from one creature to another, through which they can act upon one
another at the greatest distance. This is the basis of all sympathy and
antipathy which occurs in creatures.

15

*(from Conway's journal, a reference to a letter she received from
Newton via Henry More)*

Speaking of action at a distance, Mr. Newton calls every thing a
center, at once active and passive, acting on every other thing, as
every other thing acts on it.

16

*(a fragment of a letter written by Anne Viscountess Conway to the
Lucasian Professor of Mathematics at Cambridge University)*

with respect to god, all things are made altogether
with respect to creatures, all things are made
one after the other, one at a time.

there is an intrinsic presence between
god and creatures which transmits motion
with no lapse of time.

god is a trinity of being, word, and will,
whose will gives rise through word
to creatures and to their activity,

creation depends
on god's absolute absence
and god's real presence at the same time.

time is being
present to another.

there is no fragment of creation so small
that it cannot be divided into a smaller,
worlds within worlds within worlds.

reduce a creature to a point
beyond which it can not be divided
and it is nothing.

at bottom is nothing, but you
cannot get to the bottom
as long as you are in
the world.

17

*(from Conway's journal, a reference to a letter she received from Newton via Henry More)*

Shall we say, then, that god alone knows nothing?

18

*(a fragment of a letter written by Anne Viscountess Conway to the Lucasian Professor of Mathematics at Cambridge University)*

the infinity of creatures means
all creatures emanate into one another.

creatures are present not only to god
but also to each other.

every portion of matter is
a world of creatures containing
other worlds of creatures.

god is intimately present in all creatures.
god must always be fully present in every moment
to every moment

but creatures may be fully present only
across time: god is present.
creatures are present in time.

19

*(from Conway's journal, a reference to a letter she received from
Newton via Henry More)*

god is out of time

20

*(a fragment of a letter written by Anne Viscountess Conway to the
Lucasian Professor of Mathematics at Cambridge University)*

As I read Mr. Leibniz, the world is an infinite curve; and his monads
are internal to it. Predication is the execution of travel but not the
imposition of a world outside on an inside mind. To my mind, there
is no outside. Space is an infinite envelopment of infinite worlds, an
envelope around every perceiver. The body is not container. The
mind is not contained. Mind is where bodies go. The point is to
describe bodies going.

If God is wholly present in every instant, God goes nowhere and does
not take place.

Still, we move – from all present in a point without dimensions to
worlds in which all is present in every point. Every point an infinite

set, all, still, nowhere present, no when. And, still, each is present across a set of points, with limits.

Bodies moving make space, make time. Where there are no bodies moving, there is no space, no time.

No bodies, nobody knows.

Divide a whole and wholes, not parts, remain.

Nothing is more basic than any other thing.

# Aunt Joan
### Wally Swist

You were my mother's only sister,
and you ever so much wanted what you offered me

as gifts would then be returned to you as love;
especially when you visited after our beloved Julia died,

and you drove from Newark to Connecticut. You
sat on the bed, springs sagging, where only a few nights

previously I went to sleep beside mother, while father
was working the graveyard shift at the factory: your hair

bobby-pinned in those tight curls, the pink crocheted half
hat with a veil, only making you appear more rigid;

your white gloves lying on the lap of your dress, fingers
snapping and unsnapping the latch of your purse, pulling

small monogrammed handkerchiefs out to wipe your nose,
to wipe the tears streaming from your reddened eyes.

It was Uncle Steve whom I loved, admired. Steve,
with the dark circles under his eyes, half of his stomach

gone to cancer, patron saint of patience due to his bulwark
and steadfast loyalty to his being your husband—

always the calm voice, always the kindness emanating
in it. Whether I planned to or not, I would take Steve as

my role model, but it was you that I didn't want to become.
The possibility of that opened me like a bag of marbles

ripping; spilling the tigers, crystals, and cat's eyes that
rolled across the floor and ricocheted into the corners.

The cards you sent me, always sent air mail, were addressed
to *Master* because, as you explained to me, I wasn't old

enough yet to be a *Mister*. My thank you notes were
tardy and answered in cramped handwriting, although

it was normally fluid when I wrote anyone else. It wasn't
as if I didn't try to love you in return, it was just that

I feared I would become as needy as you, stumbling over
yourself to exhibit how much you cared for me;

and more significantly how much you hungered for me to
return your need of my affection.

By high school, the distance between us, your
age, and Steve's passing made your cards all but cease,

until even my father thought you may have died yourself,
especially since you had now lived alone.

However, it was the check you sent to me for the purpose
of my purchasing the track shoes,

that I was receptive, that I did write you back
with something other than the normal amount of uninspired

and lackluster emotion; as I practiced sprints in the backyard
wearing my wings of mercury.

Justice prevailed, I later thought, when I missed placing
third in the league meet by a half inch, believing somehow

if I had been more like Steve, and had been kinder to you,
I could have cleared that bar that wiggled up and down,

before shivering and falling to the cinders beside me.
Aunt Joan, after a lifetime of disappointments, I find you

again surfacing in my memory, and even now I sting with
guilt in my lack of attention to you in my so infrequent

recollections; but I realize that it is you with whom I have been
attempting to make amends all these years, specifically

in my choosing to love a woman who is so similar to you,
and who, like me, was unable to return my love for her.

I would be exhibiting hubris to entertain that I have met
the requisite atonement for my not reciprocating

all of what I refused that you tried to give me, since I will
never know if I have realized what my karma demands.

# What Cancer Sounds Like
### Loretta Diane Walker

This is for the welder who added another concrete step
to the stairs outside an apartment.
The flames of his drill scorched a new coat of pale green paint.

It is for the mail carrier who sorted through lives
folded and fitted into slivers of white bark.
He stuffed stern warnings, cheerful hellos,
pleading goodbyes into small metal boxes
as a box fan whirled air around his hairy ankles.

It is for those who waited at a bus stop
watching motorists revel in the cold air
streaming from car vents
while heat stepped on their toes.

It is for the truck driver who listened
to his left turn signal blink in two four meter
as he tapped his rough hands on the steering wheel.

It is for the lady who the welder apologized to for making noise,
who opened the letter left in her box—
*Results of your exam indicate an abnormal area...*

When the doctor said, *You have cancer*; she remained silent
as she listened to inverted screams echo in her lungs;
they were too loud to pass through her vocal chords.

# Close to Closure
### Ben Berman

Say someone dies and leaves an envelope
buried in her underwear drawer, sealed
and carefully inscribed: *to be opened*

*after my death.* Imagine the usual
sentiments inside – regret and gratitude,
perhaps not a complete baring of the soul,

but a distinct voice, at least, an attitude
you'd recognize—until you reach the slight
slights and buried barbs—grievances that allude

to you. The last word's not the sole word to last—
still, it would be nice if the words inside
of letters were as mutable as the letters

inside of words—if we could set aside
those hurtful asides—or turn them into clauses—
watch how the intent would shift from incite

to insight if *even if we weren't that close*
slid to the beginning of the sentence—
the *even if* evened out in the closing.

Or what if we switched the tense—to not tense?
I know we can't change what words mean
but we do have means to negotiate distance—

measures to slow us down, marks that demand
separation—so that for a few seconds
we might step back and with a clear mind

observe our surroundings through a second
lens—all that guilt that had just enveloped
us, suddenly feeling sealed off, contained.

# Her Last Letter
### Joe Blanda

On a single gray page,
in a snowy white envelope,

these few slender words—
tracks of a small bird.

"I bleed my poems
on the tooth of sorrow,

whose ruthless chewing
marks them for life.

I toss them like fish
till the beast wags

its tail or succumbs
to a glut of ingratitude

and vanishes in the shadows
that envelop my bedroom."

# Envelope

Scott Wiggerman

Her white thighs
pried open
with nimble fingers,

long enough
to slip something
in

before the deal
was sealed
with a wet tongue,

the transaction
concluded
in a pale coffin.

So Elizabethan,
this juncture
of sex and death,

once done
never to be redone,
only one chance
to do it right.

# The Ark
### Larry D. Thomas

An envelope
is an ark,
stark white,
weightless,
waiting for

the loving
lion-and-lamb
pairs of beasts,
its gangplank
readied

for the creaking
of the first pair
to board:
Acceptance
& Rejection,

so perfectly
in step each is
indistinguishable
from the other:
the end

and the beginning,
the beginning
and the end
of radiant
silence.

# envelope
### Larry D. Thomas

the thin,
white vessel
holy
with the promise
of a message:

its blankness
a snow-
covered field
of dormant
flowers:

of a pink
so pale
it's hardly
pink at all:
the pale

pink ghosts
of roses
redolent
with the promise
of the tongue.

# Envelopes Threaten

Eugene "Gene" Novogrodsky

Father nears 100.

He's angry that I pedal circles in the United States' rural middle.

He's afraid I'll die before he does.

He wants me to grow up, enter respectability.

But he crossed the Mississppi in 1936 - a honeymoon drive.

Fine for him then,

Terrible for me now.

I send him envelopes packed with corn, soy beans and wheat.

He's throws them unopened into the garbage.

He used to send me fat envelopes with baseball clippings.

I always read them.

I still send extra-postage envelopes,

While knowing that he'll forcefully throw them away.

Nothing in the mail from him, fat or thin.

# No Envelopes
### Marian O'Brien Paul

late 1970s
gas so cheap
you could collect
bottles for nickel
refunds, enough
to pump a gallon
in the starving tank
not yet a graduate
four children to feed
no envelopes to mail
out bills nor a stamp
(and even they were
cheap) tucking kids
in the car "let's have
some fun, we'll go
for a ride"
the most efficient
route mapped out
to save our gas
each child a living
envelope, allowed
to hold in hand
a statement and
a matching check
one for each store
or bank we owed
for those goods so
necessary to life

# Envelope
### Donna Pucciani

As sky is enveloped in cloud,
as cloud is dispersed in rain,

tissue-thin, prepaid,
a blue letter folded three ways

makes of itself
its own envelope.

An anachronism, this feather-light
breath of affection,

this mythic bird
of origami longing.

Whatever happened to the act
of creasing carefully the page,

licking the gummed edge
just so,

sealing a secret bliss
across an ocean?

# November Passage
### Blair Cooper

Busy, chattering as they move
head first down trunks, nuthatches.
They know something we don't
as we sit in chairs we brought out
on the deck of our vacation house
this mild autumn day, ignoring
the urgency signaled by birds.

Winter can wait. We read in the sun,
sort through mail. Across the valley
Mount Ascutney looks serene, content,
in shades of pale green and ultramarine.
Birch trees, white poles in mounds
of gold and burnt umber, climb
the hillside. Close by, sparse rust
leaves cling to maples.

At dusk, a chill wind blows in
and torn envelopes rise up from
the bamboo table, swirl with brown
leaves above our heads as we pull
chairs inside. Clouds waft in low
over the mountain's face, and we
huddle around the fireplace, watch
the start of winter through windows.

In the night—mournful honking
as late migrating geese pass over.
Tomorrow we, too, will fly south
where asters still bloom purple
and the sun heats us through.

# Back of the Envelope
### Chip Dameron

You're the only one
who sends me
real letters these days

postage paid envelopes
turned inside out
cryptic notes enclosed

scribbled on today's back
your baseball epitaph
"Prince flops Jacoby soars"

# Notes on Envelope
## Found Poem from Mt. Zion's Nelson Mandela Tribute, San Antonio TX
### Kamala Platt

"For peace, you must forgive."
"Three words for Madiba: Love Peace Unity."

A South African professor, newly arrived at UTSA
says, "In South Africa, there were many students,
like me—in high school in the 80's,
in college in the 90s—who were in the struggle,
but unlike me, many of them are not with us anymore.
Many of my generation were killed in the struggle against apartheid."

And we stand to honor his words.

A Methodist pastor says:  In Ghana, a pastor told me:
"You Americans Keep Time. We, Africans Make Time."
She says, "in Honoring Mandela I want to say two things: there is
        evil in the world
that must be addressed..." and she names injustices and isms and
        violences...,
Then she says, "there were, and are, women in the struggle...
Winnie was imprisoned too..."
She says, "... anything can change," and we stand to honor her words.

And a politician says she was put out of the classroom
for not agreeing with the teacher, and we stand.

And the next speaker says, "There are more Black Men in US prisons
        today
than were ever enslaved here before...
but as Reverend Copeland said 'I remind you in the spirit of
        Mandela:
Anything can change.'"
And we stand.

Someone says: "Don't just learn about Mandela; learn from
       Mandela..."
Someone says: "San Antonio has a sister city in South Africa"—
(and I think, I've lived here near 20 years—why didn't I know?)
Someone says, "San Antonio City Council passed a resolution against
       the Klugerrand"—
(I've heard all the stories, read the histories—why didn't I know?)
And a City Council representative says: "Our children need
       Mandela's teachings!"
And we stand.

A woman reads Maya Angelou's words:
"*In the Alamo, in San Antonio, Texas, on the Golden Gate Bridge in
San Francisco, in Chicago's Loop, in New Orleans Mardi Gras, in
New York City's Times Square, we watched as the hope of Africa
sprang through the prison's doors.*"
She says Madiba's greatest gift to the world is his "ability to forgive,"
says "*we, his inheritors, will open the gates wider for
       reconciliation,
...will respond generously to [those]...on the floor of our planet.*"

And then, the oldest Tuskeegee Airman takes the pulpit.
He says, on Mandela's 95th birthday, last July,
he'd heard a poem Mandela kept in his prison cell.
The elder started reading *Invictus*, everyday
and so, honoring Madiba, he recited the poem
in Mount Zion, on Sunday afternoon.

"*I thank whatever gods may be
For my unconquerable soul.*"

And we stand.

# It's Not Delusional
### Michelle Hartman

A white washed room, eau de sausage and wood rot
mismatched chair circle and women various ages, sizes

they smell of White Diamonds, despair and Campho-phenique.
Stalker, obsessed, fixated has been used

to describe each of them at some point. Therapy
has failed, society crucifies them

they sit, shoulders drooping, eyes transfixed
on boxes in their laps, heaped to overflow

mementos, some honestly acquired, most stolen
from Tom Selleck or hunk of the day. The most envied

hold official envelops, restraining orders as badges. Today is the day
we burn our treasures, start

a new path, face dragons and other useless clichés.
Absent fathers, abusive mothers, husbands, reason

not a good excuse. In moments we will march
outside, cleanse ourselves with fire. I will not cry

as flames lick and tickle plush fake mustache. For
I know who, duct-taped enveloped, is in my cellar.

# Remembering Little Things
### Michelle Hartman

        harder these days
but the past so vivid, Technicolor
1951, Albert marched off to war
uniform crisp, grin lopsided.
Beautiful summer with primrose
filled meadows, Indian paintbrushes,
he stood there ready to go
daylight on buttons, dancing
fairy lights over thick green grass.

He did not come back, assigned
a foreign grave. A crumpled envelope
a wrinkled telegram and she
waited keeping house clean
and herself busy;
then another war, boys dropping
in a jungle just as far away.
Albert didn't come back
from that war either, although
she saw him in news reports
a tired face that never saw a razor.
Other wars followed;
little wars, strange names, Falklands, Kosovo.
He fought them all
somewhere deep down she knew
he'd never come home but the
thought grew fuzzier each day.
Slip sliding with other memories—
where is the butter knife, powder compact
slipping away pearls rolling
off a broken string of time.
Memories rolling under the sofa
enveloped by dust bunnies.

# recycling
### Christopher Kelen

on the sill in the sun
ants yet to reach
a postcard
left words facing out
discovers itself a bleached palimpsest
even the postmark came off
so that stamp and card
have more words to take
and one more journey
to make

# in heaven
### Christopher Kelen

the text of every letter
never written
all thoughts too naïve
or clever to think

it'll all be alright
it'll all be alright
that's what they say
when the end is near

in heaven
the gentle sound
of water running

in hell
a dripping tap

# The Hidden Blue Rose
### Kerry Shawn Keys

*"miracles don't make people believe,*
*it's the belief that is the miracle"*

Wild fruit carried in vest pocket, rose-hip
from cold, coastal bush, from Blue Hill is shipped
out to disseminate the bluer Adriatic, blue sky, enveloped
in a bottle, not far from Ragusa, empire of Venus.

A rowboat floats up, cut loose from the deep,
and a lady on the prowl with blue skin skin-deep,
rose flushed within, steel-blue eyes, seagreen hair,
grabs it – a Pict? but I would pick her as the evening star.

Certainly what rises here will rise again and again
outlasting any embargo, New Wave archipelago,
what rises will have arose a dozen roses over,
hardier than my heart, harder than this Rosa Rugosa.

# Mystery School
## *for Judith Soucek Ritter Leigh*
### Jane Lipman

1

Sob of the mourning dove at dawn
Fine rain floating through cherry blossoms
I dress, step into misty East Capitol Street
Flower shadows lie on the garden path
beneath exploding forsythia
moist magnolia

Wind rises—
A blizzard of petals envelops me
To be touched by spirit—
fragile translucent pink orange
wet white petals
Slain by their touch

Cherry wings drift
down twisted black trunks
Birds sing inside the petaled boughs
Cherry trees shed moonlight-
colored blossoms—
swirling around dark bare trees
that haven't yet come to leaf

Cherry lace frames the Capitol
Jefferson and Lincoln Memorials
For a moment Washington remembers
its origin   Ornamental cherries   fruit cherries
reflect in the Tidal Basin's
petaled water   fallen stars
I used to live here   It comes over me
how I love this city

There for a workshop on Ancient and Modern
Mystery Schools, Kabbalah and Masonry
held at a Scottish Rite Temple
Lodge of the Nine Muses
where elements of the Constitution were birthed
Back home in New Mexico what stays with me
are the cherry blossoms

2

When she died, my dear friend took off, didn't hang around
for even the obligatory three days
Perhaps the length and ravages of Parkinson's
*bardoed* her straight to Paradise
I hadn't thought to ask her to send me a sign
from the other side
Twenty-six days after she crossed over—
in meditation with my friend Reita—
I'm ecstatic beneath a cherry tree by the Potomac

Blossoms cocoon me in soft rain
far as the eye can see—arcing from above
carpeting the ground drifting
Love suffuses everything
I realize Judith is here this is Judith's *baraka*
and dissolve in tears
clasped in her love that blessed my life

A medicine man stopped her once near a pyramid in Mexico
said her aura was vast as the mountains
Yes, and here it is in cherry blossoms
the dew of heaven
enfolding us and the whole Tidal Basin
We're all mixed up with the blossoms
monuments, Masons
even the federal buildings

105

3

I think of Reita when Z'ev ben Shimon Halevi asked
in the D.C. workshop if there was a Buddha in the room
Reita raised not one but both her hands
mystified by the rest of us who didn't
It comes over me that when cherry blossoms fall

they fall on the ground laughing
like me right now—at how


a woman tells the Kabbalists and Masons
that she's the Buddha
Cherry blossoms, Judith, Reita and I
laugh ourselves straight to enlightenment
The Kabbalists and Masons join in
the universal jamboree
God
beholds
God

# Seasonal Affective Disorder
### Jim McGarrah

My stomach is squeezed by sadness,
a twinge of hunger minus appetite.

In front of Welty's Deli a few blocks
from the French Quarter, lawyers make
deals, bankers lose someone else's fortunes,
and cops sweep the sidewalks clear
of pick pockets, the only honest crooks.

I'm beginning to feel SAD at 8AM.
There isn't enough breeze to lift a wing
and hurry a fly off my beignet.
A child, miserable in his mother grip,
bellows like a wounded dog, a tourist
checks the tag on her rolling luggage
although we're miles from any airport.
Worst of all, there is no newspaper to read.
The Times Picayune published since 1837
is no longer printed every day.
Knowledge costs more than ignorance.

At the next table three people clash
over the sinfulness of television, grackles
form a counterpoint harmony of useless chatter
from the eaves above the Deli's sign.

This is my world this morning, and it would be nice
in these moments of sweat and despair, to believe
I'm getting what I choose, that my minor miseries
are a reflection of my own poor perspective
rather than the Sisyphean task of being human.

# belief

### Charlie Newman

hail ends rain        may be when I brush my teeth I will
once a gain know to leave in what ever tick tock I have left
news hound skull talking in elegant new year's eve cocktail chatter
and eye seizure film at 11 that past time sense doesn't recognize soft
voices reveal    linger    die in a snow of narrow experience
dreams
evaporate in mastery    in bible    in guaranteed witness victimzen
nirvana in a tide of purpose [*or so it seems*]
      unrepentant scribbler of sure-handed stiletto ruthlessness
      a cadaver mumbling silver tongued spirals of self-centered
lust    savagery    sweat  and occasional good intentions
mirroring cancelled tv show versions of gutter Shakespeare almost
insight of kindred spirits vying for a way out    for dumps of deposed
axegrinders spread out against continuously unravelling expectorations
silence
      ecstasy
      purity
      trench confessions in quiet public places and still end less
ever lasting reruins pile on freeze frame sorrows
      [*or not*]
judgers of men        jailhouse for get me nots    but no ticket home

# Letter Received from a Boy in Kenya
*transcribed by* Elizabeth Raby

Thanking my dear, to speak like that one
me was very happy. Birthday is good day
and very nice day.

Birthday me was a small me
clean like a moon.

Birthday are many people and very happy
and cooking many food like potatoes, rice,
cabbage, juice and e.t.c.

Thank, my dear, to give money. Give
goat, sheep and cow.

One day birthday me was gone to Nairobi Show.
I look animals like big snake, zebra, buffalo,
lion and cheetah. I was do the same and me
was possession 3 marks four and ninety.

Me was a good and very happy. And mother for
me is very good. Was cook a good food and to eat.
And to eat fruit like orange, mango, carrot, avocado
and pawpaw.

I am very happy and very good. Home has many
animals like cow, goat, sheep, camel, dog, and pig.

Home was near the hill and near the river
and under the road and on the road many cars to gone
like bus, car, lorries, and motorcars.

Thanking my dear in the birthday for me.
Thank God we bless you,

Parmuya

# Sealed, Unsealed
### Elizabeth Raby

Why am I always looking
backward?  The pile
of envelopes—two cent stamps,
G. Washington's confident
left profile—I happened upon again
this week, addressed to my father
in my mother's long gone
but so familiar hand—inside,
her circumspect love letters.
She did not save his replies.
Already she the one to tidy up,
to sort and toss. And still
another envelope, postmarked
Cho-sen 1929, a good
engraving of the Korean hotel,
four fancy stamps, 1 yellow, 3 red,
addressed in my father's sure scrawl
home to his parents in Nebraska.
Everything is spotted, foxed brown
and crumbling, box after box
in the garage. I am stuck
in old times while other poets
leap forward into new forms.

# Envelope and Envelop:  A Brief History

### Carol Coffee Reposa

His two profiles
Facing opposite directions,
Janus must have wrought
These uneasy twins
While he was guarding
His gates and doorways,
Watching what came through
Or went out:  mists wreathing
Barren hills, softening their crags
And filling their depths,
Or rain sheathing the desert
In a healing sheet of gray.
Maybe he saw a herald triumphant
Unroll his scroll
To proclaim victory afar,
Another leap from his lathered horse
To announce a plague in the East
Enfolding the city in fear.

In later times
He might have noticed
The mailman delivering
Thin windowed envelopes,
Their sickly yellow
Containing words
That wrapped the world in tears
Like acid rain or Oklahoma dust,
But sometimes
The messenger might have brought
Creamy containers
Of parties, weddings, births,
Perhaps an award
Enveloping all
In warmth

Holding off the cold, the dark
Like a down comforter
On a night of January sleet.

# Remembering the Envelope
### Margaret Van Every

The heart, fueled with anticipation,
picked up its pace as the hand
entered the box, withdrew the contents.
The envelope was foreplay to the rest,
bearing the scent of the sender,
the careful flourishes of his hand,
address and return address (just in case).

A human sorter in a brick and mortar plant
would move this message on to its destined home,
despite inclement weather, we were told.
Sometimes he'd pronounce a letter *DEAD*,
owing to an illegible scrawl or absent stamp.
It would mingle then forever in a mass grave
with other letters whose future was cut short.

Most envelopes, still crisp and clean,
would find their way to the addressee,
delivered by a man walking the block,
lugging a sack of mail on his back.
The miracle ended only when a relic
called a *letter opener* sliced through
the top fold of the sealed missive,
exposing the contents to the prying light.

Envelope factories now are going broke
and no one has a use for decent penmanship.
Harbinger of a dying civilization that loathes
words, communication, and the epistolary art,
the envelope is a near defunct species,
a soon-to-be fossil of the pre-electronic age.

# Deliverance

Margaret Van Every

Foot and fist embossed on the belly,
time came when the womb had had
its fill of you, your punch and kick.
The membrane that once swaddled
you so sweetly, now was a shrink-wrapped
garment binding foot against face.
Coiled too tight, you ached to unfold
like buds, leaves, and wings.

But humans
cannot uncoil with balletic grace
like nature's other tight new
things.  The solo journey to light,
so crushing and hot, delivers the fetus
by force and presages future travel
to unknowable states of being.

# Dream Letter
### Glen Sorestad

The envelope had a postal box
in Fort Qu'Appelle and the name
of the sender was Ferguson—
just Ferguson, nothing else.
I had dreamed this, of course.
It was a handwritten request
for a copy of one of my books
and when I awoke, the writer's
distinctive script was fixed in my mind.
The letter, not much more
than a note, really, had been rerouted
from an old address and hand-delivered,
though I couldn't recall the face
of the one who delivered it.

What interests me this morning
is that this dream is so un-dreamlike,
the careful script etched in my mind.
I could duplicate it with ease, even now.
I don't know any Ferguson.
Nor anyone in Fort Qu'Appelle.

You'd think that in a dream
a letter would bring a request,
or announcement so bizarre,
so cryptic it would have to be
decoded by experts; yet here I am
with a request so mundane
that it has lodged in my recall
like a cedar sliver under a fingernail.

There must be a reason I have
been visited by such a dream.
Would you interpret it for me?

For someone like me with such
scant dream-recall beyond waking,
this dream has me here waiting—
for the letter I'm now convinced
must surely be on its way. Ferguson,
do you still want that book?

# Zombie Envelopes
## Suzanne Seed

my escalating lists
are scrawled on envelopes
filled with oceans of ephemera
info, backup odd stray stats and facts
raucous, whirly squirrels of this and that
hopefully corralled for reference
to endlessly proliferating tasks
that segue into more
lists and notes, yet more begetting more
while less and less gets crossed off, and yet more
eager notes fill angry envelopes
landlocked travelers repurposed to
cage these tasks that now envelop me
in swarms of zombie envelopes, a pack
that beats me back like Alice, info-owned
each list demanding to be first of all
and always more is added than is done
my captive life encapsulated here
no freedom but to toss the lot, explode
them into flying bits of phantom mail...

and into the midst of this incipient fit
suddenly from a friend from far away
comes an email with an image of
the best post office that there ever was
a dazzling tower blitzed with a mural of
deft mail-planes swanning through bright swoops of clouds
a Futurist mosaic, symbol of
all correspondences that ever were
a glittering launch for airborne messages
a clerestory built with walls of sky
of tesserated, glass-mosaic'd walls
picturing planes that mount the air to take
mail out to everywhere and everyone
who ever mailed a letter anywhere...

it's in Liguria, this tower that is
filled with such bright, exploding clouds put there
by Futurists, who, one can only hope
given this scene's explosive, crackling style
did not share other Futurists' mad bent
for solving problems by exploding them
dissolving function into raw escape
devolving this tower's luminosity
into a rain of glass and spinning planes
and "liberated" floating envelopes
fluttering forever here like birds
amid the languid, luxe, Ligurian light
that streams from all the windows of this tower...

but no, this postal masterpiece remains
its aircraft safe, eternal in their flight
not wind nor rain nor dark of night shall stop
these painted planes from their eternal rounds...
it must be my own mind providing scenes
of raining envelopes, like whirling birds
scraping the sun-soaked air of this bright tower
speaking of my own longing to escape
in reckless waste from duty's dailyness...
not an option really, and so how
can I escape my envelopes? perhaps
I'll write some poems on them, new lists of poems
and fold them into paper planes and aim
each at the heart of every ought and should
set dailyness to music, make new lists
of only what I'm surely born to do
lists that lift my envelopes beyond
their earthbound and domesticated state
that launch them out, refolded, to become
wings now set free

# Entre Chien et Loup
### Angela Narciso Torres

More than tearing open the cream envelope
or hearing the shush of linen paper

between eager fingers, more than the rush
of ink-spattered words, there's the waiting—

or so romantics tell us, that expansive breath
held as if underwater for what seems forever,

each cell filled to bursting with oxygen—
for a lover's letter to arrive. Like that cold

January dreaming of your first kiss, lips
parted half-asleep in class or practicing

scales on the piano, something inside
ripens to almost breaking. Anyone

observing how magnolia buds flush
before they speak in white flame

will recognize the wish to linger
in airports or train stations, prolonging

that final glimpse, or the urge to pause
on a bridge watching dusk's vacillations.

*Entre chien et loup,* the French say,
implying that all we know of heaven

is the eyelash between day
and night, between dog and wolf.

# Subject: Posted
### Jamie Stern

Picked strawberries—
If I could get them to your quarry
Before spoiling—and Lillet on the rocks
Would be better than this.
A letter is durable of course. It won't
Interrupt a swim and
It needs no refrigeration.

But the lack of juice is a problem
And it can't really be shared.
Worse still, it won't stain
Your fingers red.

So when you open this
Envelope, think
Red fingers,
Stones warm on your back,
And sweetness
You can swallow whole.

# Mirror
### Rosanne Sterne

It looks whole,
this physical body,
shell of skin, cells, follicles,
weathered to ripe
by dark suns of roiling seas.

The mirror sees
the fine accumulated lines
of each expression,
scratch scars, squint tracks, smile's claws,
the blind eye.

The mirror sees
a merely visible surface,
largest organ, wane of collagen,
quick glimpse of concern.

And, oh, but what the mirror cannot see—
the scarred heart,
lapsing resilience,
fatigue's collapsing bulwark,
creak and pain of movement,
piles of sealed scripts,
smudged envelopes,
journals rusted shut, locked dreams,
hard days recorded—

Or the drooping cardboard boxes
of memory,
frazzled pages of words,
thick dictionaries thrown open to the word *jewel*,
desperately begging the sky,
blue with reason,
for just one more poem.

# Valentine, Then
### Rosanne Sterne

in the morning
we assembled our
angry troops to open

cards, pink and blood-red envelopes
laid out on the lemon-oiled teak table,
orderly, like my father

demanded, names scrawled
in cursive, bruise-blue or black
ballpoint ink, flaps lightly licked or tucked—

until the year
one name was missing
from the front of any

wide rectangular
face, among the faithfully
penned—mine—

which engendered the insane
dash, cigarette dangling, in our robin's egg
blue finned plymouth valiant,

to the rexall drug with
the crazy, accusing pharmacist
where my mother

grabbed the fanciest
valentine, with a folded
middle that popped

up a dozen overflowing rose bouquets,
the kind we were never allowed to

buy—too expensive—

now the yellowed card burns
its hole in my drooping box of childhood
ephemera, among troll dolls and rabbits' feet,

roses folded inward, hard
reminder of how little one small child
mattered.

# Thinking Better of it
## Sarah Webb

It started with an envelope so fat somebody had taped it shut to hold
in what turned out to be $1,113 in bills and 42 cents in coins. The
address said only IRS (in crooked letters) but the Post Office had
delivered it promptly. Log it in, said his supervisor—and raised his
voice to carry—Log them all in. Sam looked up at that. Everyone
had one. Rachel had three. She showed him a letter at break. I am so
sorry, it said. No signature. His hadn't had a note. In the afternoon
there were more, boxes more. Had Investigation launched a
campaign? It was far worse than that, he discovered, as he fumbled
for the tip at the sandwich shop. Give the waitress an extra dollar, he
thought, you stiffed her last week. He watched his hand pull out a
twenty and a one. Seven times he'd stiffed her. On the drive home, a
line of cars at the police station. A motorist backed up to let him
through. There were clippers on the front step he hadn't seen in
years, and in the garage the lawn mower Benny borrowed last
summer. He'd brushed the grass off it. A former president stuttered
on the news. H-heck no, there were never any weapons. Told Dick,
but he... And the new one, Let me be clear. It's a mess! If I'd held out
for a single-payer system like I wanted, but, no, I had to be
compromising, had to be "listening." He moved his hands in air
quotes. Don't do it, don't do it! Sam pleaded with himself, but his
hand was reaching for his phone. It was dialing his ex-wife's number.

# Incantation
### Neal Whitman

when bills went unpaid
one month too many
rent, utilities ... you name it
no job, no hope
an envelope in the mail
no, not another warning or threat
no, in it five C-notes
no letter, no message
but the postmark gave him away
we served together
not hard to track him down
oh, my ... in hospice care
blue-green
winter twilight
your nurse gently knocks twice
visiting hours are over
it's time

>*in dim light the stream*
>*that falls over the edges*
>*is both still and moving*
>*stir twice*
>*oil of doubt with water of faith*
>*time before, time after*
>*the Beginning and the End*
>*Let there be light*

# Poetry for Sale

*(on reading III. Nature. XXXVII. A Thunder-Storm by Emily Dickinson)*
### Neal Whitman

Emily Dickinson would send her poems to the editor of *The Atlantic*,
  Thomas Wentworth Higginson.
He never published a single one in her lifetime.
Instead, he passed her missives to friends,
  thinking they would be amused.
A spinster in Amherst, the daughter of Squire Edward Dickinson.
Dressed in white.
  How quaint.

Now on the Internet.
Four pages, on 8 x 10 notepaper, folded in half,
  presumably to fit in an envelope.
"A Thunder-Storm," mailed to Higginson in 1873.
Its last owner Mrs. Gretchen Fiske Warren,
  once president of the New England Poetry Club.

What did Mr. Higginson find to
  devalue, disparage, disregard?

In five four-line stanzas, we see and hear:
Wind rocked.
Leaves unhooked.
Wagons quickened.
Cattle fled.
Her father's tree quartered.

Strong language. True words.
This woman knew her home and our landscape.
Oh, and the price for "her hand"? $85,000.

# Emily Dickinson's Envelopes

Al Zolynas

Besides neatly stitched fascicles,
bundled and saved for
presumed posterity,
Emily practiced a frugal husbandry
where paper was concerned, penciled
poems on envelopes unhinged
and splayed out from their folded forms.
She built her own lines to conform
to their triangular flaps and rectangles
as if the secret of envelopes—
those carriers of love and anguish—
told her all she needed to know
in this world about containment
and revelation.

# Beautiful
### Dana Heifetz

But I still can turn the wheel
and go back. Your words, your voice
saying over the phone, embarrassed, *it's me.*
Indeed, it was *you.* And me, *so very much me*
you said, I was captured. Immediately.
And how hopeful I was
to hear your voice, to read your words,
to see your face softening as I said *it's me.*

Could I be blamed
for all the rest?

Call it as you wish. I insist: beautiful.
It was, is, simply beautiful.

# Substance
### Ann Howells

Atop the mesa
soaked in riotous sun
she walks on shells
of a vanished sea.
>> Underline *vanished.*

Strong westerly winds
bring hail—just think—
ice falling in the desert.
>> Underline *just think.*

Chamisa, caliche, arroyo.
>> Underline all of these.

Bits of his speech:
jasper and feldspar,
meteorites and tektites,
giant yucca forests.
Something shifts, words
tumble her tongue:
*agate* and *sotol.* She feels
cosseted, enveloped.
>> Underline *cosseted.*
>> Circle *enveloped.*

# The Vegetarian
## Joseph Trombatore

In this scene of
shadow & antici
pation let's apply
raw sienna burnt
umber someone
is taking a drag
off a cigarette the
lighting is low no
flickering candle
no gulf coast breeze
in fact this one is
wrapped around
an email request
for a poem about
an envelope being
enveloped a subject
which I can't imagine
writing about they
are made up of 10
parts seal adhesive
top flap top fold
throat (O hummingbird
orange trumpet vine)
side flap side fold
shoulder (O how
Veronica Lake)
bottom flap seam
overlap bottom fold
back & face (the ones
your friends put on
when out in heavy
traffic) I couldn't
submit I mean I
can't imagine a

chapbook or whole
collection about en
velopes you see that's
the way I write with
a certain subject mat
ter in mind don't want
one of my poems out
there like an orphan
stranded on a desert
island a freckled-faced
red head without sun
screen a doubting
Thomas just before
his fingers well you know...

# About the Contributors

## The Editor

Jonas Zdanys, a bilingual poet and translator, is the author of forty-three other books, forty of them collections of poetry, written in English and in Lithuanian, and translations from the Lithuanian. He has taught at the State University of New York and at Yale University, where he held a number of administrative positions and was a Scholar-in-Residence in the Yale Center for Russian and East European Studies. He served for more than a decade as the state of Connecticut's Chief Academic Officer and is currently Professor of English at Sacred Heart University. More at jonaszdanys.org

## The Poets

Kyle Anderson was a winner of the 2014 VIA *Poetry on the Move* contest. His poems have also been published in *Voices De La Luna*, *San Antonio Express News*, and *The Enigmatist*. He currently teaches English to high school students in the San Antonio area.

Walter Bargen has published sixteen books of poetry. His most recent books are *Days Like This Are Necessary: New & Selected Poems* (2009), *Endearing Ruins/Liebenswerte Ruinen* (2012), and *Trouble Behind Glass Doors* (2013). He was appointed the first poet laureate of Missouri (2008-2009). www.walterbargen.com

Alan Berecka's poetry recently appeared in the *San Antonio Express* and then shortly thereafter at the bottom of countless bird cages. His latest book, *With Our Baggage*, was released by Lamar University Press in July 2013. He is not sure he can claim that he works for a living, but he puts in his time as a reference librarian at Del Mar College in Corpus Christi, Texas.

Ben Berman's first book, *Strange Borderlands* (Able Muse Press), was a finalist for the Massachusetts Book Award. He has received numerous honors from the New England Poetry Club and fellowships from the Massachusetts Cultural Council and Somerville Arts Council. He teaches in the Boston area and is the Co-Poetry Editor at Solstice Literary Journal.

Joe Blanda lives in Austin, Texas, where he makes a living as an editor and musician. His poems have appeared most recently in the *Texas Poetry Calendar 2014*, *The Enigmatist*, the anthology *Lifting the Sky: Southwestern Haiku & Haiga* (HuffingtonPost.com), and on San Antonio buses via the city's Poetry on the Move program. They've also been nominated for two Pushcart Prizes. His songs can be heard at www.CDBaby.com and www.Folkwine.net.

Donna Bowling's poetry has appeared in the *Texas Poetry Calendar*, *The San Antonio Express News*, the *Baylor House of Poetry*, *Peace Words*, *Blue Hole*, and *Windhover*. She co-authored the non-fiction book *Reclaiming Civility in the Public Square: Ten Rules That Work*.

Cynthia Wolfe Boynton's background includes more than fifteen years as a regular correspondent for *The New York Times* and nine years as editor and publishing director of *Better Health* magazine. Her two most recent plays, *Right Time to Say I Love You* and *Dear Prudence*, both made their premieres in New York City, just steps off Broadway, at the 2011 and 2013 United Solo Theatre Festival, and were recognized as top scripts. *Right Time* continued with performances that took her to Brighton, England, and one of the largest theater festivals in the world. A Connecticut resident, Cindy is also an English and communications instructor at the Yale School of Medicine and Housatonic Community College, as well as host of the weekly Literary New England Radio Show podcast. Fascinated by history and drawn to telling stories that connect the past and present, Cindy has written two books for The History Press, *Remarkable Women of Hartford* published in March 2014 and *Connecticut Witch Trials: The First Panic in the New World* published in September 2014. Her website is www.cindywolfeboynton.com.

Jerry Bradley, the 2015 winner of the Boswell Poetry Prize, is University Professor of English at Lamar University. He is the author of 6 books including 3 books of poetry: *Simple Versions of Disaster*, *The Importance of Elsewhere*, and *Crownfeathers and Effigies*. A member of the Texas Institute of Letters, he has published in many literary magazines including *New England Review*, *American Literary Review*, *Modern Poetry Studies*, *Poetry Magazine*, and *Southern Humanities Review*. Bradley is poetry editor of *Concho River Review* and is past-president of the Conference of College Teachers of English, the Texas Association of Creative Writing Teachers, and the Southwest Popular and American Culture Association, which endows a writing award in his name. More information is available on his Wikipedia page and personal website www.jerrybradley.net.

David Breeden has published widely. His latest collection is *They Played for Timelessness (with chips of when)* from Vacpoetry. He blogs at www.wayofoneness.wordpress.com.

Lauren Camp is the author of two volumes of poetry, most recently *The Dailiness*, winner of the National Federation of Presswomen 2014 Poetry Book Prize and a *World Literature Today* "Editor's Pick." "Letter to Baghdad" is included in her third book, *One Hundred Hungers*, which was selected by David Wojahn for the Dorset Prize, and will be published by Tupelo Press in 2016. Her poems have appeared in *Brilliant Corners*, *Beloit Poetry Journal*, *Linebreak*, *Nimrod*, *J Journal*, and elsewhere. She hosts "Audio Saucepan," a global music/poetry program on Santa Fe Public Radio, and writes the blog *Which Silk Shirt*. www.laurencamp.com.

Blair Cooper lives in Santa Fe, New Mexico, where she paints and writes poetry. She has published in various journals, which include *El Ojito*, *The New Mexico Poetry Review*, *Adobe Walls*, *Lummox*, and *Sin Fronteras*, where her poems have frequently appeared. She and her husband sometimes visit Vermont, a very different environment for them but one that often influences her poetry.

Sherry Craven taught high school Spanish and college English. Her poetry collection *Standing at the Window* was published by Virtual Artists Collective. She has published short fiction, creative nonfiction, and poetry in numerous journals and anthologies and received the Conference of College Teachers of English Poetry Award. She is retired, lives in East Texas, and continues to write.

Chip Dameron has published five collections of poetry, most recently *Tropical Green* from Wings Press, and has placed individual poems in a number of literary magazines, including *Taos Review, Mudfish, Borderlands,* and *Hayden's Ferry Review.* He lives in Brownsville, Texas.

Barbara Daniels' *Rose Fever* was published by WordTech Press and her chapbooks *Black Sails* and *Quinn & Marie* by Casa de Cinco Hermanas. She received two Individual Artist Fellowships for her poetry from the New Jersey State Council on the Arts and earned an MA at New York University and an MFA in poetry at Vermont College. Her chapbook, *The Woman Who Tries to Believe,* won the Quentin R. Howard Prize from Wind Publications. Her poems have appeared in *Mid-American Review, WomenArts Quarterly Journal, Sugar Mule, The Literary Review,* and many other journals.

Charles Douthat's first book of poems, *Blue for Oceans,* won the L.L. Winship/ PEN New England Award as the best book of poetry published in 2010 by a New England writer. His poems have appeared online in *Poetry Daily, Verse Daily* and in many magazines and journals. Three poems from *Blue for Oceans* were featured on Garrison Keillor's *Writers Almanac.* He graduated from Stanford University and practices law in New Haven, Connecticut. Learn more at charlesdouthat.com

Jeanie Greensfelder, the author of *Biting The Apple* (Penciled In, 2012), grew up in St. Louis, Missouri. A psychologist, she seeks to understand herself and others on this shared journey, filled, as Joseph Campbell wrote, with sorrowful joys and joyful sorrows. She now lives in San Luis Obispo, California. Her poems have been published in *American Life in Poetry, Askew, Orbis, Echoes, Grand, Kaleidoscope, Porter Gulch Review, Poetic Medicine Journal, Riptide, Falling Star, and Vine Leaves.* Poems can be seen also at slocoastjournal.com.

Michelle Hartman's work can be found *Crannog, Poetry Quarterly, The Pedestal Magazine, Raleigh Review, San Pedro River Review, Pacific Review, Concho River Review, RiverSedge, Illya's Honey* as well as over forty other journals and ten anthologies. Her work appears overseas in Ireland, Germany, Australia, Canada and Nepal. She is a multiple Pushcart nominee. Her poetry book, *Disenchanted and Disgruntled,* is from Lamar University Press. She is also the editor for the online journal *Red River Review* and holds a BS in Political Science-Pre Law from Texas Wesleyan University as well as a Certificate in Paralegal studies.

Dana Heifetz is an Israeli poet and writer of fiction as well as a philosopher, human rights lawyer, and editor of non-fiction, whose short stories and poems (in Hebrew) have been published in various Israeli journals and in several Virtual Artists Collective (vacpoetry) projects.

Ann Howells's poetry has recently appeared in *Calyx, Crannog* (Ire) and *Free State Review.* She serves on the board of Dallas Poets Community and has edited its journal, *Illya's Honey,* since 1999. Her chapbook, *Black Crow in Flight,* was published by Main Street Rag Publishing (2007). Another chapbook, *the Rosebud Diaries,* was published in limited edition by Willet Press (2012). She has been nominated twice for both the Pushcart Prize and Best of the Net.

Christopher (Kit) Kelen is a well-known Australian poet, scholar and visual artist, and a Professor at the University of Macau, where he has taught Literature and Creative Writing for the last twelve years. Volumes of Kit Kelen's poetry have been published in Chinese, Portuguese, Italian, Swedish and Filipino. An Indonesian volume is in preparation. The most recent of Kelen's dozen English language poetry books are *China Years—New and Selected Poems* and *a pocket kit*. For the last several years Kelen has been facilitating the translation of Chinese poetry into English and Australian poets into Chinese, projects which have so far produced a dozen large scale bilingual anthologies. Kelen has published two scholarly volumes about poetry: *Poetry, Consciousness, Community* (Rodopi 2009) and *City of Poets – Exploring Macao Poetry Today* (ASM, 2009). Kelen's theoretical study of national songs, *Anthem Quality*, is forthcoming from Intellect Press in the UK.

The fountain of Kerry Shawn Keys' poetry is in the Appalachian Mountains and urban America, but the roots go worldwide. From 1998 to 2000, he taught translation theory and creative composition as a Fulbright Associate Professor at the University of Vilnius. He has dozens of books to his credit, including translations from Portuguese (*Requiem*, L do Ivo, 2011) and Lithuanian, and his own poems informed by America and Europe, and Brazil and India (Peace Corps) where he lived for considerable time. His work ranges from theatre-dance pieces to flamenco to meditations on the Tao Te Ching and is often lyrical with intense ontological concerns. Of late, he has been writing prose *wonderscripts* and plays. A children's book, *The Land of People*, received a Lithuanian laureate in 2008 for artwork he co-authored. He performs with the free jazz percussionist and sound-constellation artist Vladimir Tarasov; Prior Records released their CD in 2006. His most recent book is *Night Flight* (poems), 2012. Keys received the Robert H. Winner Memorial Award from the Poetry Society of America in 1992, and in 2005 a National Endowment for the Arts Literature Fellowship. He received a Translation Laureate Award from the Lithuanian Writers Union in 2003. In 2011, two of his books of translations from the Lithuanian were published: *Bootleg Copy* (Laurynas Katkus) and *Still Life* (Sonata Paliulytė). Keys is also the English-language editor of the *Lithuanian Holocaust Atlas*, 2011. He was a Senior Fulbright Research grantee for African-Brazilian studies and is a member of the Lithuanian Writers Union and PEN. Selected poems have appeared in Czech, English, and Lithuanian. Currently, Keys is Poet-in-Residence for Summer Literary Seminars Lithuania (SLS Lithuania). He also writes a quarterly column, *Republic of Uzupis:*

*Crossroads of World Poetry, Dispatch,* for Poetry International, San Diego State University.

Jane Lipman's first full-length poetry collection, *On the Back Porch of the Moon* (Black Swan Editions, 2012), won the 2013 NM-AZ Book Award for Poetry Book and a 2013 NM Press Women's Award. Her chapbooks, *The Rapture of Tulips* and *White Crow's Secret Life*, both from Pudding House Publications, were finalists for NM Book Awards in 2009 and 2010, respectively.

Jim McGarrah's poems and essays have appeared most recently in *Bayou Magazine, Chamber 4, Cincinnati Review, Elixir Magazine,* and *North American Review.* He is the author of three books of poetry, *Running the Voodoo Down,* which won a book award from Elixir Press in 2003, *When the Stars Go Dark,* which became part of Main Street Rag's Select Poetry Series in 2009, and from Ink Brush press, *Breakfast at Denny's* (2013). He has also written a memoir of the Vietnam War entitled *A Temporary Sort of Peace* (Indiana Historical Society Press, 2007) that won the Eric Hoffer Award for Legacy Nonfiction, and *The End of an Era,* a nonfiction account of life in the American counter-culture during the 1960's and 1970's, published in 2011 by Ink Brush Press. McGarrah has been nominated for a Pushcart Prize and was a finalist twice in the James Hearst Poetry Contest.

Gary Metras has published three books of poems and thirteen chapbooks, most recently *Two Bloods: Fly Fishing Poems* (winner of the Split Oak Press Chapbook Award, 2010). Poems, essays, and reviews have appeared in *Boston Review of Books, English Journal, Poetry, Poetry East, Poetry Salzburg Review,* and *Small Press Review.* His new book of poems, *Captive in the Here,* is due out from Cervena Barva Press in 2014.

Born and raised in Sofia, Bulgaria, Katia Mitova moved to Chicago in 1993. She is the author of two books of poetry, *The Human Shell* (original Bulgarian title *Tlenna Obvivka,* Pero, 1994) and *Dream Diary* (Virtual Artists Collective 2013), as well as of a doctoral dissertation on the dialogical character of literary creativity (University of Chicago, 2005). She has translated ten books from Polish and English into Bulgarian, including poetry by Czeslaw Milosz and Mark Strand. She is a professional faculty at The Chicago School of Professional Psychology and also teaches literature and philosophy in the Basic Program of Liberal Education for Adults at Graham School, University of Chicago.

Charlie Newman was born in Newark, NJ, 5.17.43. Punk and industrial damage bands since '79. 4 books. 1 chapbook. 4 CDs. Various publications and collections. Has read in Chicago, NYC, London, etc. with David Amram, the Viking Hillbilly Apocalypse Review, Mouth and Hands, and ZOOTSUITBEATNICK! Hosted a radio show and 2 venues in Chicago. Now writes and reads and reads and writes.

Eugene "Gene" Novogrodsky of Brownsville, Texas, is a founding member of the 13-year old bilingual Narciso Martinez Cultural Arts Center Writers Forum in San Benito, Texas. He has lived on the Mexican/United States border for 26 years. He enjoys the slices of life existence delivers, and also enjoys writing about them. His motto is "Peace Bread Health," "Paz Pan Salud."

Vasilina Orlova was born in the village of Dunnai in the Russian Far East in 1979. She has lived in Vladivostok, Moscow, and London, and is now based in Austin, Texas. She holds a Ph.D. in Philosophy and is the author of seven novels in Russian, among them *The Voice of Fine Stillness*, *The Wilderness*, and *The Supper of a Praying Mantis*. She has also published several books of prose and poetry, including *Yesterday*, *The Wilderness*, and *Quartet*. She is the recipient of several Russian literary awards and is a laureate of the Anton Delvig Prize for the poetry book *Barefoot* (2008). She has written in English since 2012. Her first book in the language is a collection of poetry titled *Contemporary Bestiary*. Her poetry and prose have been translated into English, French, Spanish, Bulgarian, Ukrainian, and Russian.

A literature and creative writing teacher for more than 25 years, Marian O'Brien Paul has a Ph.D. in Writing and English Literature. Her most recently published poetry includes Line 7 in the *Gathering Poem* (Dublin, Ireland, Feb. 2014–50 lines chosen from 8000 submitted by people of Irish descent across the world). Poems published in 2013 include "Cahokia Mounds, Illinois" in *The Midwest Prairie Review*, "Legacy of Apple Trees" at www.sphericaltabby.com, and "Listen" for the WTFrack 2013 project at http://www.borderbend.org/8/post/2013/08/listen.html. Her poems can be found in the "Poetic Asides" column, *Writer's Digest* and *The Stony Thursday Book* (Limerick, Ireland, 2010). In the past thirty years her poems appeared in journals, magazines, e-zines, and in *Virginia Woolf and the Arts: Selected Papers from the Sixth Annual Conference on Virginia Woolf* ("The Voyage Out: a Poem" 1997).

Kornelijus Platelis is a Lithuanian poet, translator, essayist, editor, and government official who served as Lithuania's Minister of Education, as Vice Minister of Culture, and as Deputy Mayor of the city of Druskininkai. He has served also as Editor-in-Chief of the Vaga Publishing House and, since 2001, as editor-in-chief of *Literatura ir menas* (Literature and Culture), Lithuania's principal arts and cultural journal. His first book, *Words and Days*, appeared in 1980 and he has since published several collections of poems, essays, and translations, as well as a commentary on the Bible. His work has been translated into twenty-four world languages; the most recent translation was Jonas Zdanys' English translation of *Solitary Architectures* (Lamar University Press, 2014) . He was awarded the Lithuanian National Award for Culture and Art in 2002.

Kamala Platt, Ph.D., M.F.A., is an author (*Weedslover: Ten Years in the Shadow of September*, 2014, *On the Line*, Wings Press, 2010, compiler: *Kinientos*, Wordsworth, 1992,). She is an artist, independent scholar and a *profesora* in South Texas and at The Meadowlark Center in Kansas. She has many poems on envelopes and hopes to collect and bind them, someday soon.

Mark Podesta studies literature and writing at Sacred Heart University. He is at work on his first full-length collection.

Donna Pucciani, a Chicago-based poet, has published poetry in the U.S., Europe, Australia and Asia in such diverse journals as *International Poetry Review, The Pedestal, Shi Chao Poetry, Spoon River Poetry, Journal of the American Medical Association,* and *Christianity and Literature.* Her work has been translated into Italian, Chinese and Japanese. Her books include *The Other Side of Thunder, Jumping Off the Train, Chasing the Saints,* and *To Sip Darjeeling at Dawn.* A four-time Pushcart nominee, she has won awards from the Illinois Arts Council, The National Federation of State Poetry Societies, and Poetry on the Lake.

Elizabeth Raby has been rummaging through boxes of old envelopes for several years. Her memoir of four generations of her family, *Ransomed Voices,* was published by Red Mountain Press of Santa Fe, New Mexico, in October 2013. www.redmountainpress.us Three collections of her poetry were published by Virtual Artists Collective. www.vacpoetry.org

The poems, reviews, and essays of Carol Coffee Reposa have appeared or are forthcoming in *The Atlanta Review, The Evansville Review, The Formalist, Coal City Review, Southwestern American Literature, The Texas Observer, Valparaiso Review,* and other journals and anthologies. Author of four books of poetry—*At the Border: Winter Lights, The Green Room, Facts of Life,* and *Underground Musicians*—she also has received three Pushcart Prize nominations along with three Fulbright-Hays Fellowships for study in Russia, Peru, Ecuador, and Mexico. She has twice made the short list for Texas Poet Laureate. A professor emeritus of English at San Antonio College, she now serves as poetry editor of *Voices de la Luna.*

Susan Rooke is a two-time Pushcart Prize nominee who lives in Austin, Texas. She has recent or forthcoming poems in *San Pedro River Review, U.S.1 Worksheets, Melancholy Hyperbole, Mojave*

*River Review*, *Texas Poetry Calendar 2014*, and elsewhere. She soon will publish her novel *The Space Between*, the first of a planned fantasy series.

Steven Schroeder is a poet and visual artist who has spent many years moonlighting as a philosophy professor. His most recent collections are *Turn* and *Raging for the Exit* (with David Breeden). His translation of *The Daodejing* (with David Breeden and Wally Swist), is new from Lamar University Press. More at stevenschroeder.org.

Suzanne Seed's poems are often op-eds (in agreement with what Ferlinghetti once suggested poetry needed to be in his time). They've been published in *Chicago Magazine*, the *Chicago Sun-Times*, and other such venues. In addition, she has received awards for books of interviews/photojournalism (American Library Association, Chicago Women in Publishing, Chicago Book Clinic), for critical writing (Logan Award), and for a peace poster done for the Shoshin Society in commemoration of the anniversary of the Hiroshima bombing. She is a member of PEN, the Authors' Guild, and the National Writers Union, and serves as Honorable Advisor for Tokyo/Osaka Designers Gakuin College/Photographic College. Her writing, whatever the medium, is about the relationship between religion/politics, the trance of cultural belonging, and violence.

Vivian Shipley has published five chapbooks and nine books of poetry. She is a two-time recipient of the Paterson Award for Sustained Literary Achievement, and two of her books—*Gleanings: Old Poems, New Poems* and *When There Is No Shore*—were nominated for the Pulitzer Prize. Additional honors include the Library of Congress's Connecticut Lifetime Achievement Award for Service to the Literary Community, the Connecticut Book Award for Poetry, the Lucille Medwick Prize from the Poetry Society of America, the Robert Frost Foundation Poetry Prize, the Ann Stanford Poetry Prize from the University of Southern California, the Marble Faun Poetry Prize from the William Faulkner Society, the Daniel Varoujan Prize from the New England Poetry Club, the

Hart Crane Prize from Kent State, the Connecticut Press Club Prize for Best Creative Writing, and the Binghamton University Milt Kessler Poetry Book Award. Editor of the award-winning *Connecticut Review*, she is Connecticut State University Distinguished Professor at Southern Connecticut State University, where she was named Faculty Scholar in 2000, 2005 and 2008. She has a Ph.D. from Vanderbilt University and is a member of the University of Kentucky Hall of Fame for Distinguished Alumni. Vivian lives in North Haven, Connecticut with her husband, Ed Harris.

Glen Sorestad is a well-known Canadian poet who lives in Saskatoon. His poems have appeared in literary magazines all over North America and other countries. They have been translated and published as well in seven languages. His poems have appeared in over sixty anthologies and textbooks as well as in his more than twenty books and chapbooks of poems published over the years.

Jamie Stern is an attorney in New York City, where she lives with her two sons. Her first volume of poetry, *Chasing Steam*, was published by Virtual Artists Collective in 2013. She has co-published two poetry anthologies in honor of Marie Ponsot, *Still Against War* (2011) and *Still Against War II* (2012). She is a member of the Board of Poets House, a literary center and poetry library in lower Manhattan.

Rosanne Sterne is a poet, watercolorist and flutist whose poetry has been widely published in literary journals, including *Artisan, Journal of Poetry Therapy, Long Island Quarterly, New Mexico Poetry Review, Progenitor*, and *Santa Fe Literary Review*. Her first chapbook of poems, *Dancing in the Gaps*, was published in 2010 by Finishing Line Press. Rosanne is a graduate of Harvard University and recipient of the Harvard David McCord Prize for creativity. She holds an M.B.A. from the University of Denver and works as a consultant to foundations with a special focus on arts and culture. She lives in Colorado.

Bill Sullivan is professor emeritus at Keene State College, New Hampshire, where he taught courses in American literature and American studies. He is a co-author of *Modern American Poetry* and *Containing Multitudes: Poetry in the United States since 1950*. He also co-produced *"Here Am I,"* a documentary film on the life of Jonathan Daniels, a slain civil rights worker. The film aired on numerous PBS stations. His poems have appeared in *Babel Fruit, Perigee, New Verse News, Origami Poems, The Providence Journal,* and *Westerly Sun*. He now resides in Westerly, Rhode Island.

Wally Swist has published twenty books and chapbooks of poetry, often in letterpress limited editions. His book, *Huang Po and the Dimensions of Love*, was selected by Yusef Komunyakaa as a co-winner in the Crab Orchard Series Open Poetry Competition, and was published by Southern Illinois University Press in 2012. His book, *Winding Paths Worn through Grass*, was published by Virtual Artists Collective, of Chicago, also in 2012. He is the author of *The Friendship of Two New England Poets: Robert Frost and Robert Francis* (The Edwin Mellen Press, 2009); and as an editor he has provided commentaries for Moscow Ballet's *Great Russian Nutcracker* (Talmi Entertainment, 2012). His latest book, a new translation of *The Daodejing* of Laozi from Lamar University Press, is a collaboration with David Breeden and Steven Schroeder.

Larry D. Thomas, the 2008 Texas Poet Laureate, is a member of the Texas Institute of Letters. One of his three poems included in this anthology, "On Stationery of Light," is part of a correspondence in verse (*Wolf Tree and Agave*) currently in progress with his friend and the publisher of six of his poetry collections, Clarence Wolfshohl (El Grito del Lobo Press). Thomas's most recent poetry collections are *The Lobsterman's Dream (Poems of the Coast of Maine)*, El Grito del Lobo Press, Fulton, Missouri, 2014, and *The Goatherd*, Mouthfeel Press, El Paso, Texas, 2014. *Art Museums* is forthcoming in early 2015 from Blue Horse Press in Los Angeles, California.

J. C. Todd is author of three volumes of poems, *Nightshade, Entering Pisces* and, most recently, *What Space This Body*. Her poems have appeared in *The Paris Review*, the *Virginia Quarterly Review*, *American Poetry Review*, and other journals. Awards include a poetry fellowship from the Pennsylvania Council on the Arts, two Leeway Foundation awards, and fellowships to VCCA, the *Kunstlerhaus* at Schloss Wiepersdorf in Germany, and The Baltic Center for Writers and Translators in Visby, Sweden. Her poetry has been translated into Italian, Lithuanian, Latvian and Macedonian. She has lectured at universities in Germany for the U. S. Embassy in Berlin. As a contributing editor to the on-line journal, *The Drunken Boat*, J.C. has compiled and edited mini-anthologies of contemporary poetry in translation from Lithuania and Latvia. She is a lecturer in Creative Writing at Bryn Mawr College and for the MFA in Creative Writing Program at Rosemont College.

Judith Toler has been an editor, an English professor, faculty union organizer, artist and poet. She began writing poetry after retiring to Santa Fe, New Mexico from Rochester, New York. Since then, dozens of her poems have appeared in a variety of anthologies and literary magazines. Judith recently published a limited-edition chapbook, *Picasso's Horse*, and is currently completing another chapbook, *My Grandmother's Name Was Grace*, as well as her first full-length book of poems, *In the Shine of Broken Things* — both due for publication in 2014.

Angela Narciso Torres's first book of poetry, *Blood Orange*, won the Willow Books Literature Award for Poetry and was published by Willow Books/Aquarius Press in September 2014. A graduate of Warren Wilson MFA Program for Writers and the Harvard Graduate School of Education, Angela has received fellowships from the Illinois Arts Council, Ragdale Foundation, and Midwest Writing Center. Born in Brooklyn and raised in Manila, she currently resides in Chicago, where she serves as a senior poetry editor for RHINO.

Joseph R. Trombatore is an artist and poet whose work has appeared in *Travois: An Anthology of Texas Poetry*, *Right Hand Pointing* (online), *Journal of the American Studies Association of Texas*, and elsewhere. His poetry collection, *Screaming at Adam*, was awarded the Wings Press Chapbook Prize in 2007, and one of his poems received the 2011 Larry D. Thomas Poetry Prize (REAL, Regarding Arts & Letters). Other honors include two Pushcart Prize nominations and a Best of the Net Anthology nomination. Former Poetry Editor of *The Houston Literary Review* (online) and Founder/Publisher of the defunct online journal, *Radiant Turnstile*, he now resides in San Antonio, Texas.

Margaret Van Every lives in Mexico near Guadalajara and is the author of three books of poetry: *A Pillow Stuffed with Diamonds* (Librophilia 2011); *Saying Her Name* (Librophilia 2012), and *Holding Hands with a Stranger* (Librophilia 2014).

Mark Vinz is the author of *Mixed Blessings* (Spoon River, 1989) and of *The Work Is All, Poems by Mark Vinz* (Red Dragonfly, 2011). His work has been published in several magazines and books, most recently one in collaboration with Clarence Wolfshohl, *In Harm's Way, Poems of Childhood.*

Loretta Diane Walker is a two-time Pushcart nominee. She has published two collections of poetry. Her manuscript *Word Ghetto* won the 2011 Bluelight Press Book Award. Her work has appeared in a number of publications, including *The Concho River Review, Haight-Ashbury Literary Journal, Illya's Honey, Orbis International Journal, San Pedro River Review, The Texas Observer* and, most recently, *Red River Review* and *94 Creations.* She teaches music at Reagan Magnet School in Odessa, Texas. She received a BME from Texas Tech University and earned an MA from The University of Texas of the Permian Basin.

Sarah Webb edited poetry for twelve years for *Crosstimbers* (University of Science and Arts of Oklahoma). She co-edits the Zen arts magazine *Just This* and serves on the editorial committee of *All Roads Will Lead You Home.* Her collection *Black* (Virtual Artists Collective, 2013) was a finalist for the Oklahoma Book Award.

Neal Whitman lives in Pacific Grove, California, with his wife, Elaine. In recital, they combine his poems with her flute, and, in journals, they combine his poems with her photographs. Outside his home country, Neal's poetry has been published in Australia, Canada, Croatia, India, Israel, Japan, Romania, Serbia, and the UK. His 2014 awards include the *Oak Magazine* Minnie Memorial Award, 2nd Prize in the California Coalition of Chaparral Poets, honorable mention in the Bay (San Francisco) Area Poets Coalition, and honorable mention in the Haiku Society of America's Henderson Haiku Contest.

Scott Wiggerman is the author of two books of poetry, *Presence* and *Vegetables and Other Relationships*, and the editor of several volumes, including *Wingbeats: Exercises & Practice in Poetry*. He recently received his third Pushcart nomination. He is the founding editor of Dos Gatos Press in Austin, Texas, publisher of the *Texas Poetry Calendar,* now in its seventeenth year.

Clarence Wolfshohl is professor emeritus of English at William Woods University. He operated Timberline Press for thirty-five years until the end of 2010. His poetry and creative fiction have appeared in *Concho River Review, North Dakota Quarterly, Colere, Rattlesnake Review, Cenizo Journal, San Pedro River Review, Melic Review, Houston Literary Review, Right Hand Pointing* and *Red River Review* (online). He was featured poet in the August 2013 *Red River Review.* A chapbook of poems about Brazil, *Season of Mangos,* was published by Adastra Press (2009) and *The First Three* (2010) and *Down Highway 281* (2011) were published by El Grito del Lobo Press. *In Harm's Way: Poems of Childhood,* in collaboration with Mark Vinz, was published by El Grito del Lobo Press in early 2013. A native Texan, Wolfshohl now lives with his writing, two dogs and two cats in a nine-acre wood outside of Fulton, Missouri.

Al Zolynas was born in Austria of Lithuanian parents in 1945. After growing up in Sydney, Australia and Chicago, he lived in Salt Lake City, and in Marshall and St. Paul, Minnesota. At various times he has been a kitchen helper, lifeguard, worker in a felt factory, cab driver, road construction worker, poetry editor, and resident poet in the schools. He teaches writing and literature at Alliant International University, San Diego, holds a Ph.D., and resides with his wife in Escondido, California. Poems of his have been widely published in books and translated into Lithuanian, Spanish, Ukrainian, and Polish.

www.ingramcontent.com/pod-product-compliance
Lightning Source LLC
Chambersburg PA
CBHW021505090426
42739CB00007B/482